Ana Kinsella

Literary
DUBLIN
Landscapes

PAVILION

Explore the city's vibrant
legacy, where every street
tells a story

CONTENTS

6 BOOKSHOPS
8 The Gutter Bookshop
10 Books Upstairs
12 The Last Bookshop
14 Ulysses Rare Books
16 Chapters Bookstore
18 The Winding Stair
20 Hodges Figgis
22 Stokes Books

24 LIBRARIES
26 National Library of Ireland
30 Glasnevin Cemetery
32 Marsh's Library
34 The Chester Beatty Library

36 THEATRES
38 The Abbey Theatre
40 The Gate Theatre

42 MUSEUMS
44 Irish Writers Centre
46 Museum of Literature Ireland
      (MoLI) at Newman House
50 St Patrick's Cathedral
52 National Gallery of Ireland
54 The James Joyce Centre

58 WRITERS
60 Oscar Wilde
62 William Butler Yeats
66 Patrick Kavanagh
68 John Berryman
70 Eavan Boland
72 John McGahern
74 Colm Tóibín
76 Brendan Behan
80 Maeve Brennan
82 Maeve Binchy
84 Elizabeth Bowen
86 Ludwig Wittgenstein
88 Edna O'Brien
92 Mary Lavin
94 Bram Stoker
96 Flann O'Brien
98 Samuel Beckett
100 John Banville

102 PLACES
104 River Liffey
108 Trinity College Dublin
112 Baggot Street
114 Rathmines and Rathgar
116 St Stephen's Green
118 Summerhill

120 Pearse Street and Westland Row
122 The Irish Times, Tara Street
124 Stoneybatter

126 JAMES JOYCE'S DUBLIN
128 James Joyce
130 Sandycove
132 Finn's Hotel
133 15 Usher's Island
134 Sweny's
136 Chapelizod

138 PUBS AND CAFÉS
140 Bewley's Café
142 Mulligan's
144 Toners
148 The Shelbourne Hotel
150 The Bailey
151 McDaid's
152 The Palace Bar
154 Davy Byrnes
156 Wynn's Hotel
158 The Duke

160 Bibliography

LEFT A bronze statue of the eccentric poet, novelist and dramatist Oliver Goldsmith who graduated from Trinity College in 1749. Made by J.H. Foley, it stands outside Trinity College's front gate.

ABOVE Libraries and bookshops: your passport to new worlds.

FOREWORD

When it comes to discovering a new city, there's no substitute for the real thing. No guidebook can truly replicate the sensation of walking a city's streets and taking it in for yourself. But for Dublin, where I grew up and where I live now, the body of literature produced in and about the city provides something else for the curious reader. It provides a way for the reader to map Dublin without ever necessarily stepping foot there.

I grew up in Dublin and studied here, leaving in my early twenties to live and work in London as a writer. I spent twelve years away from my hometown before returning to live here once again. During the time I was away, I focused my own writing on place and people, and in the process, I became more and more drawn to the literature of the city where I'd grown up. I sought out the Irish authors I'd neglected to read as a teenager, and through their writing I began to put together a more complex idea of Dublin than the one I'd built purely through my own experience of living there.

It's a kind of mythology, the thing we create in our minds through reading. Reading the works of authors like Anne Enright, Eavan Boland and John Banville was akin to learning an alternate history of my hometown, something that is personal and also public at the same time. In my mind, I began to put together a new image of the city. When I moved home in my thirties, I brought with me the many-layered ideas of Dublin that I had developed during my time away.

Literature can be a way of travelling without moving an inch. The work of Dublin's writers has long been a draw for visitors to the city from all over the world. For many readers, it is James Joyce's *Ulysses* that acts as a skeleton key to Dublin. It's a book that took me a long time to read, and I did so in chunks over the course of a decade or more. The slowness of my consumption suited the text because as I got older and got to know my hometown on different levels, Joyce's sprawling novel revealed more and more of the city to me.

His depiction of a single day in Dublin, 16 June 1904, through the eyes of Leopold Bloom and Stephen Dedalus, is probably the best and deepest representation of any city in literature. And once read, the visitor to

Dublin will inevitably see traces of *Ulysses* everywhere, in the Martello towers that dot the coastline, in the names of streets walked by Bloom, and in the handful of shopfronts, pubs and establishments that have remained mostly unchanged since 1904. Joyce's writing on Dublin is a kind of mythology, but one that feels particularly concrete in reality. The map he makes of Dublin fits the territory snugly.

But visitors to Dublin don't need to have read *Ulysses* to appreciate the role that literature plays in the city. Here, literature is as intrinsic as history itself and indeed the two are linked in Ireland in an important way. Struggles for Irish political autonomy in the nineteenth and twentieth centuries were accompanied by artistic ambitions to establish a national literature and dramatic tradition. William Butler Yeats and Lady Gregory had this in mind when they founded Dublin's Abbey Theatre in 1904, which they stated was intended 'to bring upon the stage the deeper emotions of Ireland'. This was a clarion call for writers and artists in Ireland at the time.

The legacy of this ambition has permeated into the decades since, too. It created generations of writers and artists who saw the forging of a uniquely Irish cultural tradition as part of an important political project. This is not to say that their output was uniform; on the contrary, this ambition gave rise to myriad different kinds of 'Irish' literature, from Samuel Beckett's pitch-black humour to Edna O'Brien's crisp, candid chronicles of shame and sacrifice.

All of this comes to bear when one walks the streets of Dublin. Whether you have lived here your whole life or whether it's your first visit, your amble through Dublin is accompanied by the spectres of generations of writers who took the city as setting or subject matter. A pint ordered in a traditional Dublin pub may be drunk underneath framed black-and-white photographs of the poets and artists who drank in that same pub decades earlier. Visiting the Grand Canal near Baggot Street Bridge, one might call to mind the poetry of Patrick Kavanagh, who took this location as a major source of inspiration. In his poem 'Epic', recounting a land dispute in his native County Monaghan, Kavanagh compares the argument to the Trojan War, quoting Homer as saying 'I made the *Iliad* from such / A local row'. After he moved from Monaghan to Ballsbridge in 1939, Kavanagh maintained his focus on the local, turning ordinary Dublin vistas and street scenes into the stuff of great art in his poetry.

How long should one spend discovering Dublin? It's a difficult question to answer. For some of the city's writers, a whole lifetime wasn't long enough to get to know every aspect of the place, to luxuriate in it and to appreciate it for what it is. For others, like James Joyce, Edna O'Brien or Samuel Beckett, it was a case of getting out as soon as possible. Many of Dublin's greatest writers created their work in a kind of self-imposed exile, writing back to the place that could never truly offer them a sense of home. The avid reader could spend weeks here retracing the steps of their favourite bygone Irish writers – but when time is of the essence, a few days might have to suffice, and can indeed be enough to cover many of the city's sights.

Whatever the itinerary, one will find that history and literature are close at hand, even though the city has changed much in recent decades and might be near-unrecognisable to a time-travelling Yeats or Joyce. The writers who call Dublin home today have to contend with different kinds of urban problems compared to their antecedents: cost of living and the housing crisis make the city more hostile to those pursuing the poorly-paid practice of writing.

Nonetheless, Dublin is still alive with literature, in the form of a well-funded calendar of events, journals and writing groups, and of course, the world's greatest bookshops. In this city, literature is not kept behind glass for the privilege of a rarified few. It is everywhere: in the streets and shopfronts mentioned in *Ulysses*, in the Trinity cobblestones evocative of Sally Rooney's first two novels, in the River Liffey with its three bridges named for three of Dublin's writers, in the windows of historic bookshops and in the corridors of the city's museums and libraries. It is for everyone: readers and writers of all sorts, anyone who has ever been minded to pick up a book and discover the new world contained within.

BOOK

SHOPS

LEFT The bookshop's name pays homage to one of Dublin's most famous sons, Oscar Wilde.

BOTTOM LEFT Lively Temple Bar in the heart of Dublin is the Gutter Bookshop's home.

THE GUTTER BOOKSHOP

Cow's Lane, Temple Bar, Dublin 8

Located on a pleasant corner in the alleys of Temple Bar, the Gutter Bookshop has the feeling of a friendly neighbourhood bookshop right in the heart of the city. That's a conscious effort on the part of the shop's staff, who run regular book clubs for customers, as well as hosting Q&As and readings from authors. Established in 2009, the Gutter Bookshop takes its name from Oscar Wilde's adage, taken from his play *Lady Windermere's Fan*, 'We are all in the gutter, but some of us are looking at the stars.'

Gutter has a sister bookshop in the seaside suburb of Dalkey. Both started life as independent shops before becoming part of the small Irish chain Dubray Books in 2022, a decision made by former owner Bob Johnston so he would have more time to write books of his own. The shop maintains its name, its independent and friendly spirit, as well as its varied selection of Irish and international fiction, non-fiction and children's books.

BOOKS UPSTAIRS

17 D'Olier Street, Dublin 2

Books Upstairs started life not in its current premises on D'Olier Street, but in a premises about a kilometre away on South King Street. In May 1978, Maurice Earls and Enda O'Doherty set up shop in a former hairdresser's above a furrier. Bookshelves took the place of wash basins and mirrors, and Books Upstairs became known for stocking not only literature, history and politics but also genres that Earls and O'Doherty believed to be underrepresented in Ireland, like literary criticism, philosophy and queer literature, along with a wide array of journals.

After a spell in the George's Street Arcade in the 1980s, Books Upstairs moved to a pretty Georgian building on College Green and then to its current address in 2015 – a larger space with a sunlit, WiFi-free café on the first floor. Despite its many addresses over the years, Books Upstairs has always maintained a steadfast commitment to Irish literature, with particularly well-stocked selections of poetry, essays and memoir.

LEFT Vintage cover designs add to the appeal of rummaging for treasure.

BOTTOM LEFT A large pavement display hints at the choice within.

THE LAST BOOKSHOP

61 Camden Street Lower, Dublin 2

There's a certain kind of second-hand bookshop that book lovers can't resist: a place where books are stacked high from floor to ceiling, with plenty of chaotic piles to comb through at leisure. Tables set outside to catch the eyes of passers-by, and of course, the rich and lingering smell of the printed page, a sensation that encapsulates much of the experience of reading a physical book. The Last Bookshop is possibly Dublin's greatest example of this kind of bookshop. Hours can be spent rooting through the stock here, which includes a wide Irish literature and history section. The back catalogues of many of Ireland's greatest novelists, dramatists and poets are to be found here, as well as sections dedicated to religion, science and general fiction. Tucked at the back of the shop is a door leading to a verdant courtyard. Home to the ever-popular Cake Café, this beloved spot is the ideal place to dip into your newest purchases over a mug of tea.

ABOVE Chaos, or curation? Bring an open mind and sharp eyes.

LEFT Regulars come for the cafe hidden at the back of the store.

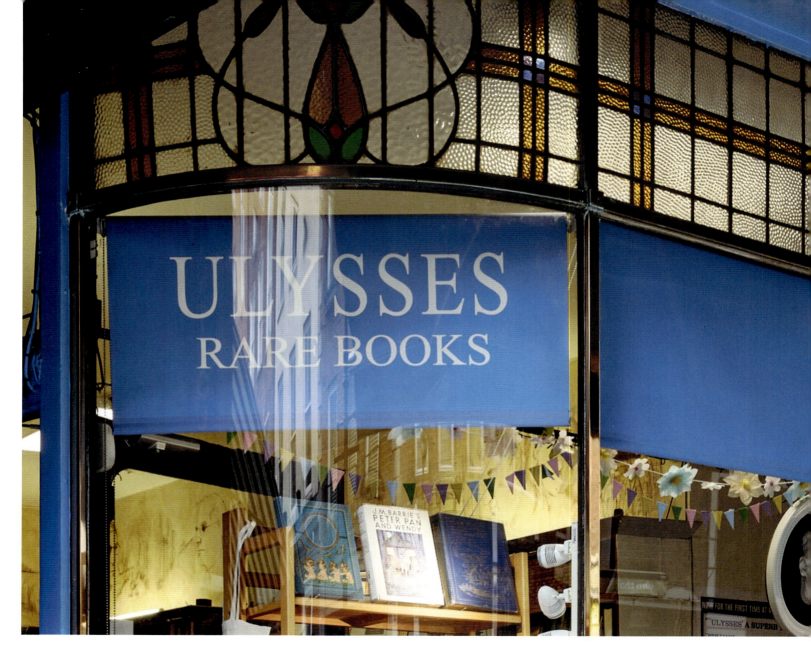

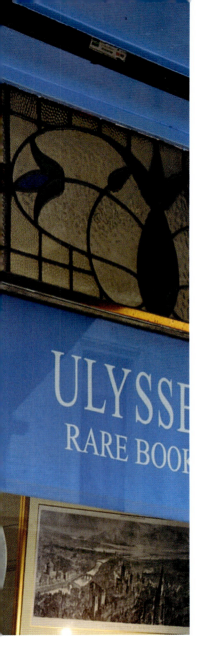

LEFT Dublin's most important rare-book dealer is instantly recognizable.

ABOVE RIGHT James Joyce surveys the shop named after his most famous work of fiction.

BELOW RIGHT Rare editions beckon for collectors of both books and maps.

ULYSSES RARE BOOKS

10 Duke Street, Dublin 2

With its pretty blue awning and plate-glass shopfront, Ulysses Rare Books is one of the finest antiquarian bookshops in Dublin. Formerly known as Cathach Books and run by the Cunningham family since its establishment by Enda Cunningham in 1969, this bookshop has been located on Duke Street since 1988. Ulysses Rare Books focuses on twentieth-century Irish literature, as well as maps dating back to the seventeenth century. Beautiful rare editions by authors such as Edna O'Brien, James Joyce, Seamus Heaney and Oscar Wilde can be found on the shelves, along with books in the Irish language. Copies of Thomas Kinsella's 1969 translation of the Irish-language epic *Táin Bó Cúailnge*, with haunting illustrations by the Irish modernist painter Louis Le Brocquy, will often pass through the shop before being snapped up by collectors, who pay over €1,000 for a first edition.

LEFT The glass-fronted Chapters Bookstore sits on Parnell Street.

RIGHT New publications by Irish authors are proudly promoted here.

CHAPTERS BOOKSTORE

Ivy Exchange, Parnell Street, Dublin 1

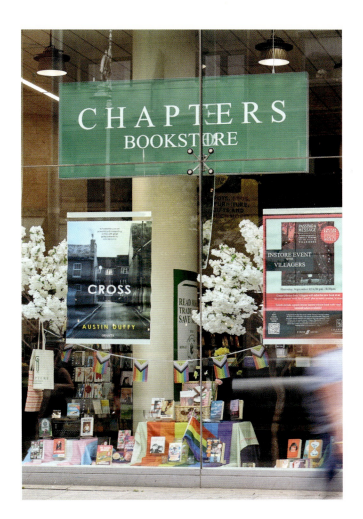

Covering over 3,000 square metres, the sprawling Chapters Bookstore on Parnell Street is a mecca for readers in search of a bargain. Here, the latest releases sit next to marked-down remaindered books and plenty of second-hand volumes, too. Armchairs are placed around the aisles, so readers can rest while browsing. Every autumn, students arrive here with reading list in hand, ready to stock up their shelves for a new term. Trade-ins are welcome, giving the shop the feeling of a reader's marketplace, where books themselves are both currency and end product.

Plans to shutter the shop in 2022 brought the city's shoppers out in droves, buying up discounted stock and talking of the special place Chapters holds in their memories. The outpouring of support from readers worked, and management decided to keep this Dublin institution open for a new generation of book lovers.

LEFT Spelled out in newsprint for newcomers to Dublin!

OPPOSITE A poetic name and riverside position make The Winding Stair a must-visit.

THE WINDING STAIR

40 Lower Ormond Quay, Dublin 1

Nestled on the north side of the River Liffey, overlooking the cast-iron Ha'penny Bridge, the Winding Stair is one of the oldest bookshops in Dublin. With its name taken from a poem by W.B. Yeats (and alluding to the distinctive eighteenth-century staircase inside), its literary credentials ring loud and clear. In the eighties and nineties, the bookshop-slash-café was a bohemian hangout popular with writers and artists. This was helped by the fact that the offices of *In Dublin* magazine, which published writers like Colm Tóibín, Fintan O'Toole and Nell McCafferty, were located in the building's basement.

Today, the café upstairs has evolved into an upmarket and well-regarded restaurant, with tables underneath tall Georgian windows looking out over the river below. The eclectic bookshop remains on the ground floor, where the tables are crowded with novels, volumes of poetry and books on history and Irish culture.

LEFT AND BELOW The store is mentioned in works by James Joyce and Sally Rooney, among others.

RIGHT Hodges Figgis is one of the oldest bookshops still trading.

HODGES FIGGIS

56–8 Dawson Street, Dublin 2

Hodges Figgis claims to be one of the oldest bookshops in the world, clocking in at around 250 years of continuous bookselling. In that time, it has had many different addresses in the wider Grafton Street area, but its contemporary store on Dawson Street is the one that today's Dubliners will know and associate with the Hodges Figgis name. The green nineteenth-century façade at 56–8 Dawson Street, with its curved glass shopfront windows, has an old-world look and inside its four floors are packed with books on every topic imaginable. The ambience here is relaxed and quiet, and the shelves are often packed with browsers lingering over a book at leisure.

The longevity of Hodges Figgis as a central Dublin bookshop has meant that its name pops up in all sorts of Irish literature: in *Ulysses*, Stephen Dedalus remembers an attractive young woman he gave a 'keen glance' to while she browsed the Hodges Figgis window, while in Sally Rooney's *Conversations with Friends* it is a destination for Christmas shopping. The bookshop's proximity to Trinity College helps maintain its reputation among Dublin's readers, and its upper levels are also a popular spot for book launches.

ABOVE The passage outside the shop is important display space.

RIGHT The tiled floor joins the interior to the market beyond.

RIGHT AND BELOW Look carefully for a first edition among the second-hand volumes.

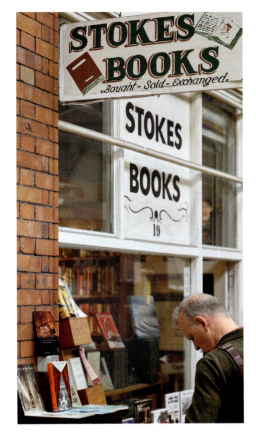

STOKES BOOKS

19 Market Arcade, South Great George's Street, Dublin 2

One of the only covered arcades in Dublin's city centre, the George's Street Arcade has been home to various bookshops and record stores over the years. Stokes Books has occupied a slim section of the passageway here since 1989. Outside the small shop, tables and shelves crowded with books pull in curious passers-by, and on entering the space inside, one finds floor-to-ceiling shelves heaving with second-hand and antiquarian editions. First editions nestle on shelves dedicated to authors like Samuel Beckett, James Joyce and Iris Murdoch. Browsing this quiet, calm bookshop, one feels the space has remained unchanged throughout the years, despite the ever-evolving hubbub on the city streets outside.

LIBRA

IRIES

LEFT The entrance rotunda.

BELOW LEFT Wrought-iron gates and railings, in the same style as the parliament building next door.

OPPOSITE The library was built in classical style, signifying its importance to the city.

NATIONAL LIBRARY OF IRELAND

7–8 Kildare Street, Dublin 2

The National Library of Ireland is located in a purpose-built building adjacent to Leinster House, which houses the Oireachtas (the Irish parliament). This alone can tell the visitor to Dublin something of the importance of books and literature to the Irish national psyche. On its opening in 1890, the *Dublin Evening Mail* described the new National Library as 'a magnificent pile'. It is indeed a prized example of Victorian architectural magnificence in Dublin today: The library's entrance hall is an elegant rotunda, lined with twelve stained-glass windows and with colourful mosaic flooring that includes depictions of the library's symbol, the owl.

The library's vast collection of over 12 million objects includes the archives of Irish writers such as Seamus Heaney, Edna O'Brien, James Joyce and President Michael D. Higgins. Reader's tickets are available for visitors who wish to study in silence in the grand D-shaped reading room, its coffered ceiling painted in shades of light blue and green. Contemporary readers on any given day might include

LEFT There are more than 12 million items in the library's collections.

BELOW LEFT Some of the 12 stained-glass windows in the entrance hall.

OPPOSITE The library houses a permanent exhibition about W.B. Yeats.

writers, historians, artists and researchers of family genealogy. The library also houses a permanent exhibition of the life and work of W.B. Yeats (see page 62). A similar exhibition drawn from the library's Seamus Heaney collection is housed around the corner, in the Bank of Ireland Cultural and Heritage Centre on Westmoreland Street.

The 'Scylla & Charybdis' episode of *Ulysses* takes place in the library. Here, Joyce features the real-life librarian T.W. Lyster, who is portrayed as being friendly and helpful to the troubled Stephen Dedalus, who has appeared in Lyster's office fresh from a nearby pub. A plaque to Lyster's memory now hangs by the entrance to the library's reading room, its text composed by his friend W.B. Yeats.

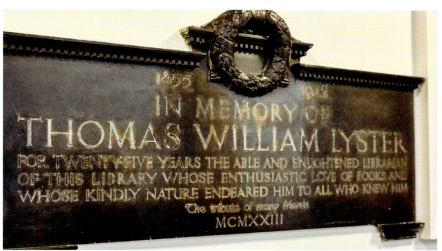

TOP Librarian Thomas Lyster is memorialized in *Ulysses*.

ABOVE Part of the mosaic floor at the entrance. Sapienta means Wisdom.

GLASNEVIN CEMETERY

Finglas Road, Glasnevin, Dublin 11

One and a half million Dubliners are buried in Glasnevin Cemetery, the 124-acre site in north Dublin that has been the final resting place for many in the city since its establishment in 1832. Traditionally Glasnevin was where Catholic Dubliners were buried, and being so crucial to the city, it may be unsurprising to learn that the cemetery is the setting for the 'Hades' episode of *Ulysses*, in which Leopold Bloom wanders through Glasnevin Cemetery after attending the funeral of Paddy Dignam there on the morning of 16 June. As Bloom passes among the graves, he thinks about life and death, reflecting on how those buried souls he is surrounded by once walked around Dublin as he does now. Each year on Bloomsday (see page 129), costumed Joyceans arrive at Glasnevin Cemetery to re-enact Leopold Bloom's visit.

All year round, though, the cemetery is open to the public. As well as being home to the graves of many Irish revolutionaries and political figures, it is also the resting site of writers including Brendan Behan, the poet Gerard Manley Hopkins and Christy Brown, author of *My Left Foot*.

LEFT The library is named for Archbishop Marsh, its founder.

BELOW LEFT Bay markers in keeping with the grandeur of the bookshelves.

BOTTOM LEFT Bram (Abraham) Stoker's signature in the visiting book.

MARSH'S LIBRARY

St Patrick's Close, Dublin 8

Tucked just behind St Patrick's Cathedral, hidden from the street, is Dublin's oldest public library. Marsh's Library was established by Archbishop Narcissus Marsh in 1707 and is still open to the public, both visitors who wish to look around and scholars alike. Inside, its two galleries are broadly similar to how they were in Archbishop Marsh's day: elegant and imposing bays of shelves that house over 10,000 books, maps and other printed matter.

Bram Stoker consulted the poetry, history and geography collections here as a young man in 1866, and library records show that James Joyce signed in twice in 1902. Though it is not known exactly what books Joyce consulted, he did mention Marsh's Library in Stephen Hero, Finnegans Wake and Ulysses. Like other scholars who visited the library, Stoker and Joyce would have sat in the Old Reading Room. Today, this bright room is used by staff to work on conserving books from the collection. The Second Gallery has one notable feature that speaks to Dublin's bygone reading public: three caged bays for readers, so staff could ensure books were not stolen. These cages were introduced in the wake of a spate of disappearances in the 1770s. The stacks are said to be haunted by Marsh's own ghost still, who comes at night to look through the books as if in search of some eternal truth.

ABOVE The building opened in 1707.

LEFT The 18th-century shelving is beautifully preserved.

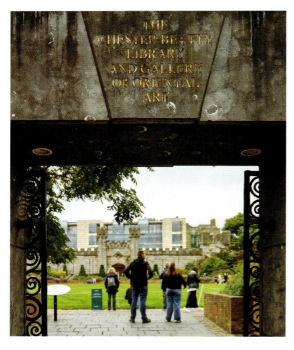

THE CHESTER BEATTY LIBRARY

Dublin Castle, Dame Street, Dublin 2

An American mining tycoon spends a lifetime building a collection of important manuscripts and artefacts, and towards the end of his life, they wind up in a museum of his own making in Dublin. That's the story of Alfred Chester Beatty and his eponymous library. Known as 'the King of Copper', Beatty collected everything from Marie Antoinette's furniture to Egyptian papyrus from the fourth century. He moved to Ireland in 1950 aged 75 and, keen to establish a legacy of his own, opened his library and museum on Shrewsbury Road in Ballsbridge in 1954. The Chester Beatty Library showcased his rare books, manuscripts, painted miniatures and early prints to the public, who received the benefit of the wealthy man's passion for collecting.

After his death in 1968, the extensive collection was left to the Irish people in Beatty's will. He was buried at Glasnevin Cemetery and was the first private citizen in Irish history to be accorded a state funeral. Today the Chester Beatty, as the museum and library is known, is housed within the grounds of Dublin Castle, where everything from sixteenth-century editions of Homer's Odyssey to Japanese Buddhist texts can be viewed.

THEA

TRES

LEFT The theatre was founded by
W.B. Yeats and Lady Gregory in 1904.

OPPOSITE Today the theatre is
housed in a 1960s design by architect
Michael Scott.

THE ABBEY THEATRE

26–7 Lower Abbey Street, Dublin 1

It's hard to imagine a poet with loftier ambitions than W.B.
Yeats (see page 62) at the turn of the twentieth century.
In a city packed with theatres, Yeats wished for a place to
stage his own verse drama, plays that would speak to the very
consciousness of the country. Ireland at the time was riven
by political strife and disagreement, and many nationalists
held dreams of creating a literary culture that was distinctly
Irish, drawing upon local interests and the mythology of the
country itself. With Lady Gregory, an Anglo-Irish dramatist
with an interest in folklore, Yeats opened the Abbey Theatre
as Ireland's national theatre in December 1904. In the
theatre's galvanizing manifesto, Yeats wrote that the Abbey's
ambition was 'bring upon the stage the deeper thoughts and
emotions of Ireland'.

Three years later, riots erupted at performances of J.M.
Synge's *The Playboy of the Western World*, which audiences
took to be indecent due to its allusions to adultery. The close
links between the Abbey's cultural output and Irish politics
persisted; during the Easter Rising of 1916, the first fatality
among the Irish rebels was Sean Connolly, an actor due to
appear on the Abbey stage that very day.

THE GATE THEATRE

Cavendish Row, Parnell Square, Dublin 1

Founded in 1928 by Hilton Edwards and Micheál MacLiammóir, the Gate Theatre was an important addition to Dublin's theatre scene. Its founding mission, to introduce Irish audiences to international theatre – distinct from the purposes and aims of other contemporary theatres which wished to develop an Irish dramatic tradition – was reflective of Edwards and MacLiammóir themselves. Both men were born in England, and MacLiammóir was in fact born Alfred Lee Willmore to English parents, reinventing himself with a fully Irish ancestry on moving to Ireland during the First World War.

Edwards and MacLiammóir lived and worked together, though did not identify themselves as gay, in keeping with the cultural climate of the time.

Their home at 4 Harcourt Terrace was something of an artistic salon in the city. Around town, they became known as 'the Boys' and together were responsible for introducing a cosmopolitan and international flavour to Dublin's theatre scene through the Gate.

The Gate has occupied the former Rotunda Assembly Rooms on Parnell Square since 1930. Over the years it has developed longstanding connections to Samuel Beckett and Brian Friel, as well as to international dramatists like Harold Pinter. In 1931, a 16-year-old Orson Welles made his stage debut. Today, the theatre offers a blend of contemporary Irish drama and international talent and features in the annual Dublin Theatre Festival.

OPPOSITE LEFT The Gate, a national institution in Ireland.

OPPOSITE RIGHT Many great artists have begun their careers here.

ABOVE Former assembly rooms were repurposed to house the theatre.

MUSE

UMS

OPPOSITE The Writers Centre is a great place for a book launch or event.

RIGHT Georgian rooms repurposed for contemporary workshops and classes.

IRISH WRITERS CENTRE

19 Parnell Square, Dublin 1

Ireland's literary culture is not something that has come about by accident. The rich literary history of a city like Dublin is continued today through state support and funding for the arts. The Irish Writers Centre, housed in a Georgian townhouse on the north side of Parnell Square, is a prime example of what that looks like. Since the early nineties, the IWC has provided development resources and support for writers of every kind and at every level. On Parnell Square, upstairs classrooms are the venue for writing courses where writers take their tentative first steps towards a draft, and book launches and open mic nights are held for authors ready to share their work with the world. The IWC also holds a Novel Fair each year, introducing would-be debut authors to prospective agents and editors.

Supports like these can make a real difference to an individual author's career, but they also go a long way in ensuring Ireland has a vibrant and living literary ecosystem. From where the IWC sits at the top of Parnell Square, the future of Irish writing looks to be in safe hands.

MUSEUM OF LITERATURE IRELAND AT NEWMAN HOUSE

86 St Stephen's Green, Dublin 2

Stepping into Newman House, one can get an idea of what it was like for a young James Joyce (see page 128) to attend university here in the years between 1898 and 1902. At that time, University College Dublin was based in this adjoining pair of grand Georgian townhouses sandwiched between St Stephen's Green and the Iveagh Gardens, and students like Joyce took their seats in its ornate stucco-ceilinged rooms to study classics, arts and sciences.

But Newman House's literary heritage is not purely a thing of the distant past. With UCD having moved mostly to its modern campus at Belfield, south Dublin, in the sixties, the old Georgian buildings have taken on a new role. Today Newman House is home not to college students and lectures, but to the Museum of Literature Ireland, a collaboration between the National Library of Ireland and UCD that opened in 2019 to showcase the best of Irish literature and to bring literary culture to life. Named MoLI (pronounced 'Molly') in a nod to Molly Bloom of *Ulysses*, the museum retains its connections to Joyce, while also making space for the many rich textures of Irish writing. Rotating exhibitions on Irish authors sit alongside gems from the collections of UCD and the National Library, including Joyce's 'Copy No. 1' of *Ulysses*, as well as many manuscripts and personal letters from authors like Maeve Binchy and Edna O'Brien. New energy imbues the old walls at MoLI in the form of a lively events programme, bringing together Irish authors and poets to share their work with a contemporary audience in this most historic setting.

OPPOSITE LEFT MoLI viewed from its gardens, which join with the Iveagh Gardens at the building's rear.

ABOVE AND OPPOSITE RIGHT James Joyce's Molly Bloom is celebrated in the museum's nickname.

MUSEUMS **47**

ABOVE The telephone from Samuel Beckett's Parisian apartment.

TOP AND ABOVE Displays on the lives and works of Irish literary greats, including W.B. Yeats and Oscar Wilde.

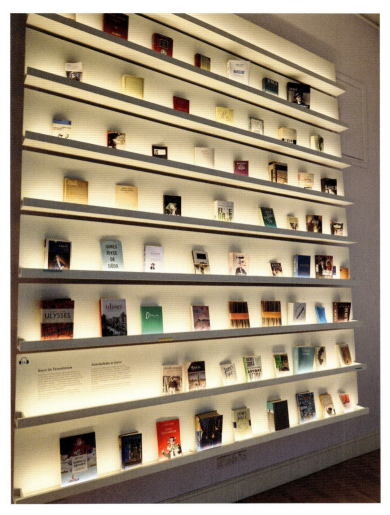

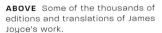

ABOVE Some of the thousands of editions and translations of James Joyce's work.

LEFT A Joycean wander through the map of Dublin.

ABOVE RIGHT Bram Stoker, author of *Dracula*.

BELOW RIGHT Accreditation for acclaimed writer and activist Brendan Behan.

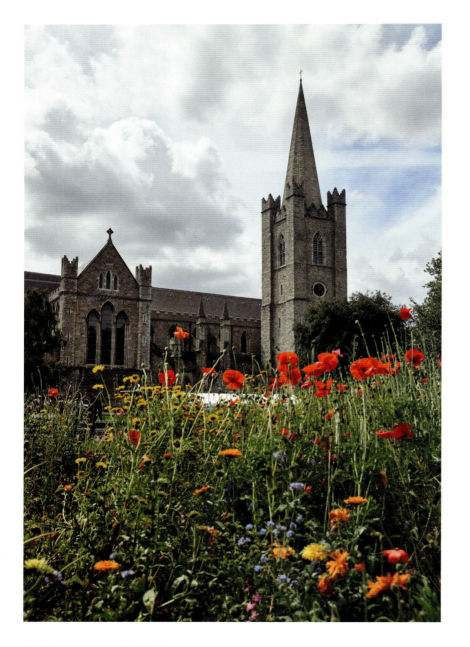

ST PATRICK'S CATHEDRAL

St Patrick's Close, Dublin 8

Jonathan Swift had a complicated relationship with his hometown of Dublin. Born in the city in 1667 and educated at Trinity College, he became a Church of Ireland priest, balancing his religious work with the writing of novels like *A Tale of a Tub* and *Gulliver's Travels*. Swift's hope was that his close political connection to the ruling class in England would land him a spot at one of the major cathedrals in England. Instead, to his disappointment, he was given the reins of St Patrick's in Dublin in 1713, where he remained Dean for over thirty years.

Swift was nevertheless an important part of Dublin city life. He was very involved in social affairs, speaking out against mistreatment of the Irish in his satire *A Modest Proposal*. When he wrote his own epitaph in Latin before his death, Swift described himself as a 'champion of liberty'. W.B. Yeats would go on to translate Swift's epitaph into an English-language poem, titled 'Swift's Epitaph'.

Swift's resting place remains in the Cathedral, which is open to the public and holds two sung services per day. In one corner of the Cathedral is a copy of *Ireland's Memorial Records*, the book containing the names of Irish soldiers who died in the First World War. Each page features an intricate illuminated border by the artist Harry Clarke, known also for his striking stained-glass windows. Charles Dickens visited the Cathedral in 1853 and noted that it was in a 'lamentable state of decay'. A restoration process would soon begin, and today it is a very fine example of Gothic architecture in Dublin, while also containing much of the city's rich literary history within its walls.

OPPOSITE Twenty-first-century planting encourages biodiversity in the churchyard.

ABOVE The Gothic Cathedral of Ireland's patron saint, Patrick.

OPPOSITE AND RIGHT The Millennium
Wing on Clare Street.

BELOW RIGHT The original building,
the heart of the National Gallery.

NATIONAL GALLERY OF IRELAND

Merrion Square West, Dublin 2

A country's national gallery is an important tool in the education of artists and writers, and Ireland's is no exception. Located on Merrion Square and part of the cluster of cultural institutions around Leinster House, the National Gallery of Ireland has been a beloved part of Irish cultural life since it was opened by the Earl of Carlisle in 1864. The Nobel Prize-winning writer George Bernard Shaw noted it as the place 'to which I owe much of the only real education I ever got as a boy in Éire', due to the time spent wandering its galleries in his childhood. He would go on to leave a third of his posthumous royalties to the Gallery, which he also described as the 'cherished asylum of my boyhood'.

Today the Gallery has expanded from its original nineteenth-century form, and new wings have opened including the Millennium Wing on Clare Street, with its striking neo-Brutalist design. Inside, the permanent collections include works by many great Irish and international artists, as well as the National Portrait Collection, which is home to commissioned portraits of contemporary writers and other figures from Irish public life. Mandy O'Neill's dual photographic portrait of Edna O'Brien captures the award-winning author once with eyes closed as she readies herself, and then once focusing intently on the camera. A colourful oil painting of best-selling novelist Marian Keyes, by Dublin-born artist Margaret Corcoran, was unveiled in 2024. Corcoran said that with her portrait of Keyes, she wished 'to paint not only a portrait but an image that spoke to the fondness of her readers both nationally and globally.'

ABOVE A place of pilgrimage for any Joyce aficionado.

LEFT The elegant building on North Great George's Street.

LEFT The famous door knocker of
7 Eccles Street, now back in place.

THE JAMES JOYCE CENTRE

35 North Great George's Street, Dublin 1

For readers of his work, the city of Dublin can sometimes seem like a living museum dedicated to James Joyce. Those who wander the city with knowledge of *Ulysses* and *Dubliners* will see traces of his writing everywhere. But for those who wish to go straight to the heart of the matter, the James Joyce Centre is a fitting first stop on the tour.

In this well-preserved townhouse on North Great George's Street, you'll find exhibitions dedicated to different aspects of Joyce's life and work. The courtyard behind the ground floor contains the original door from 7 Eccles Street, the fictional home of Leopold and Molly Bloom. When that building was torn down in the sixties, the door was saved from destruction and after being situated in The Bailey pub for some time, it is now on loan to the James Joyce Centre – and fully intact. In 1966, an American tourist stole the distinctive iron knocker, shaped like a head, believing he was saving it from destruction. In 2013 he flew back to Dublin to reunite the door with its knocker at last.

North Great George's Street itself is also a part of Joyce's lore, with the building that houses the Centre having been saved from demolition by the Joycean scholar Senator David Norris in 1982.

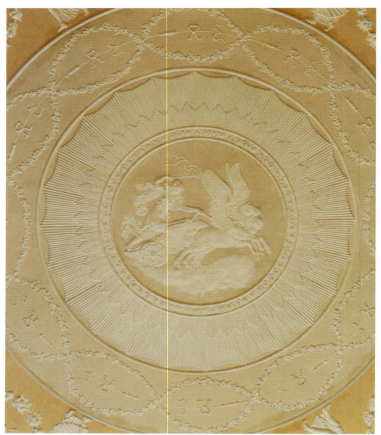

TOP LEFT The Kenmare Room hosts events and conferences as well as its permanent exhibits.

LEFT A mural by Paul Joyce, depicting scenes from *Ulysses*.

ABOVE The plasterwork is original, from the eighteenth century.

RIGHT The Maginni Room was originally the dining room of the house.

WRIT

ERS

OSCAR WILDE

Born at 21 Westland Row, Oscar Wilde grew up nearby at 1 Merrion Square before being sent to boarding school aged nine. Today, tourists flock to see a colourful statue of the writer lounging on a rock, which faces his childhood home from within Merrion Square.

Wilde returned to Dublin to study classics at Trinity, where he shared rooms in Botany Bay with his brother, Willie Wilde. His room was described by fellow students as grimy, and while Wilde was active in the university Philosophical Society, he was by all accounts not a particularly sociable student. Nonetheless, it was at Trinity that Wilde began to develop the aesthetic style that would go on to define him and his writing, aided by his studies with the scholar J.P. Mahaffy, who introduced the student Wilde to Hellenic art and inspired his enduring love of Greek culture. After studying at Oxford, Wilde went on to spend most of his adult life living in London and Paris. He would often return to Dublin for visits, though, and it was during one of these visits in 1884 when Wilde was delivering a lecture at the Gaiety Theatre that he met Constance Lloyd. Wilde and Lloyd were to marry in London later that same year.

Despite living away from Ireland, Wilde's time studying in Dublin clearly left a lasting impact on him that would persist throughout his writing career in London and Paris. That connection goes both ways, too: Wilde's lively aphorisms speak to the playfulness of Hiberno-English, and how the zippy sentence or turn of phrase has influenced what we know of Irish literature today.

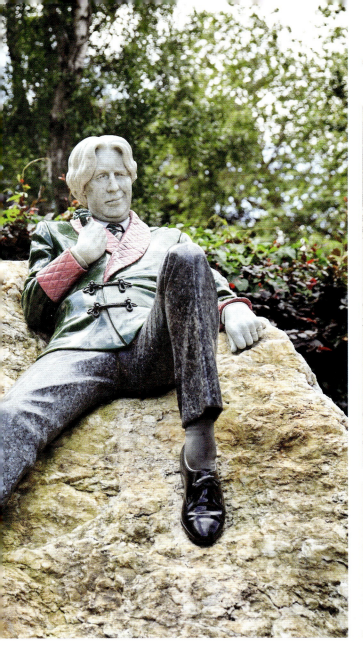

ABOVE Wilde's childhood home at Merrion Square.

FAR LEFT The dramatist memorialized in a colourful sculpture by Danny Osborne, in Merrion Square.

LEFT A plaque to Oscar's mother, the poet 'Speranza'.

WILLIAM BUTLER YEATS

If Ireland can be said to have a single national writer, one whose work is intractably linked to the country's identity, it might be W.B. Yeats. Born William Butler Yeats in the seaside suburb of Sandymount in 1865 to a notable Anglo-Irish family, Yeats grew up during a time of seismic change in Ireland. These political developments would have a lasting effect on Yeats's work, shaping the form of his poetry and his work in the theatre.

In his early twenties, Yeats met Maud Gonne, a wealthy young woman with an interest in Irish nationalism. This was the beginning of one of the great unrequited love stories of Irish history. Yeats proposed to Gonne four times over the course of twelve years and each time was turned down. She inspired many of his poems throughout his career, and in his fifties, Yeats even proposed to Gonne's daughter Iseult, who shrewdly followed her mother's example and turned him down.

Yeats's prolific poetry put him at the centre of Irish life and current affairs. His poem, 'September 1913', was one of several he wrote in response to the contemporary scandal

THIS PAGE The beach suburb of Sandymount Strand, where Yeats spent his childhood.

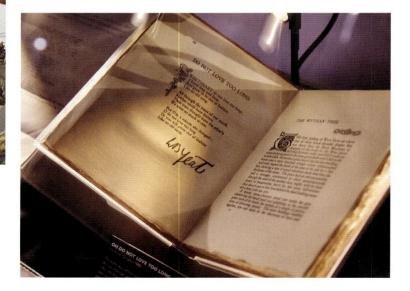

TOP W.B. Yeats's birthplace.

ABOVE The Sandymount shoreline.

FAR RIGHT AND RIGHT, ABOVE AND BELOW The life and work of Yeats celebrated at the National Library.

around the Hugh Lane bequest. Lane was an Irish art collector who bequeathed his substantial collection to the city of Dublin, on the understanding that a new building could be provided for them. The new building was blocked by local businessmen and the bureaucracy involved in the process frustrated Lane so much that he chose to leave the art to the National Gallery in London instead. Yeats's political poem on the topic, with its refrain 'Romantic Ireland's dead and gone', was published in the *Irish Times*. Poems like this, written in quick-fire response to issues that Dubliners were talking about, made Yeats more than just another poet: he was a leading figure of the day, a recognisable character who walked the city's streets and spoke of the same things they did.

Yeats lived at many addresses around central Dublin, including on St Stephen's Green and Merrion Square. At the latter, his two-minute commute brought him to work at the Seanad, the upper house of parliament where he was made a senator in 1922. Today, the Nobel Prize he won in 1923 is held nearby at the W.B. Yeats exhibition at the National Library, along with myriad manuscripts, first editions, his own passport and other ephemera. Taken together, they speak to the impact this one writer had on Irish artistic identity at a time of great change for the country.

PATRICK KAVANAGH

Patrick Kavanagh moved to Dublin in 1939, after an early life as a farmer in rural Monaghan and a brief stint in London. In doing so, he was following in the footsteps of the writers he admired most. Dublin to him was a 'literary metropolis'. At the time, having published a single collection of poetry that detailed Irish rural life, Kavanagh was hardly to know then that he too would become a major character in the city's literary landscape.

It didn't take him long to get settled. The poet soon became a regular in many of the city's literary pubs like The Palace Bar (see page 152) and The Pearl Bar, both on Fleet Street, where he met many of the poets he so admired, and was surprised to find himself treated not so much as their peer, than as an impressively learned peasant.

For years, Kavanagh cobbled together a living as a journalist and critic, while also publishing such notable poetry collections as *The Great Hunger*. Living for a long time in a bedsit at 62 Pembroke Road, Kavanagh was a part of the neighbourhood in the Baggot Street area of Dublin (see page 112). His friend Anthony Cronin described it as 'his village', reminiscent of his childhood in Monaghan. The leafy streets in this area, and the bohemian life lived there, became closely associated with Kavanagh through poems like 'Canal Bank Walk' and 'On Raglan Road'. Critics note the similarities between Kavanagh's rural poems and his Dublin work; both speak to the universe contained in the local, whether out in the countryside or on the banks of the Grand Canal in Dublin. There, a life-sized bronze sculpture of Kavanagh now rests on a bench, contemplating the water in the same way the man himself did for so many years.

OPPOSITE LEFT 62 Pembroke Road.

OPPOSITE RIGHT, AND LEFT The statue of Kavanagh by John Coll, forever sitting by Dublin's Grand Canal.

TOP AND ABOVE Raglan Road, near Kavanagh's home, where the leafy surroundings inspired new work.

JOHN BERRYMAN

When the American poet John Berryman arrived in Ireland in September 1966, he considered himself a man on a mission. In a poem addressed to W.B. Yeats, he writes that he moved to Dublin 'to have it out with you'. Berryman had long since considered himself an acolyte of Yeats, and had briefly met the older Irish poet in London while studying at Cambridge. But now Yeats was gone, and this Irish sojourn was Berryman's attempt to come to terms with that long lineage of discipleship.

The eight months Berryman spent in Dublin certainly turned out to be momentous. Taking up residence with his wife Kate in Lansdowne Park in Ballsbridge, Berryman, a prodigious drinker, fell in with a crowd of barflies that included Ronnie Drew of the folk group The Dubliners. His time spent propping up the bar led him to meet local poets and writers like Patrick Kavanagh and John Montague, as well as the actor John Hurt. During his months in Dublin, Berryman wrote that he was uninspired by the local literary scene, but he did manage to write many poems that would later be published in his major work *The Dream Songs* in 1969. *Life* magazine sent the photographer Terence Spencer and journalist Jane Howard to profile him, photographing him in Ryan's pub in Beggars Bush and making much of the boozy nature of the poet's life.

But soon it would be time for Berryman to end his Dublin sabbatical. A bad fall in early 1967 led to a brief stay in the mental hospital at Grangegorman in Stoneybatter, his experience of which informed some of the later poems in *The Dream Songs*. Like that of Yeats himself, the shadow of the city lies over these poems, pulsing through the ghostly poetic voice that Berryman employs.

THIS PAGE Ryan's Bush pub, centre of Berryman's social life during his Irish sojourn.

OPPOSITE Berryman's Dublin home, 55 Lansdowne Park.

TREE OF LIFE

A TREE ON A MOONLESS NIGHT
HAS NO SAP OR COLOUR.

IT HAS NO FLOWER AND NO FRUIT.

IT WAITS FOR THE SUN TO FIND THEM.

I CANNOT FIND YOU
IN THIS DARK HOUR
DEAR CHILD.

WAIT
FOR DAWN
TO MAKE US CLEAR TO ONE ANOTHER.

LET THE SUN
INCH ABOVE THE ROOFTOPS.

LET LOVE BE THE LIGHT THAT SHOWS AGAIN
THE BLOSSOM TO THE ROOT.

Eavan Boland

NATIONAL MATERNITY HOSPITAL
1894 - 1994

ABOVE Boland's 'Tree of Life' poem in Merrion Square.

LEFT The National Maternity Hospital, where Eavan Boland was poet-in-residence.

EAVAN BOLAND

Born in Dublin in 1944 to a diplomat father and artist mother, Eavan Boland began publishing poems while she was still a teenager, attending Trinity College Dublin. It would be the beginning of a long and fruitful career that established her as one of Ireland's leading poetic voices, and one of its most notable woman writers.

For Boland, Dublin was a 'city of shadows' – a complex and many-layered place that she moved back to in her early teens after a childhood abroad. She regarded the city as history made real, where the political abuts the personal and the private. The home she would make on the leafy Ailesbury Grove in Dundrum was the epitome of the kind of quiet suburban life she wrote of in her book of essays *Object Lessons*, and the influence of suburban domesticity is everywhere in the ordinary beauty within her poetry.

In 1994, Boland was selected as poet-in-residence at Holles Street National Maternity Hospital in the city centre during the hospital's centenary year. During her time there, she wrote a poem titled 'The Tree of Life', for a remembrance service to mark the babies that had died there over the years. This poem is now inscribed on a tablet in Merrion Square facing the hospital. Boland's poems about her hometown were collected in *A Poet's Dublin*, to mark her seventieth birthday in 2014, along with photos she had taken of the city. After her death in 2020, many prominent figures in the arts called on Trinity College to install a permanent memorial to her, celebrating her achievements as an Irish woman writer.

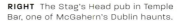
TOP McGahern owned a 'little house' in Stonybatter.

ABOVE St Patrick's College, Drumcondra, where McGahern taught.

JOHN McGAHERN

John McGahern's novels of Irish rural life have given him a deep association with the countryside, and in particular the areas of Co. Leitrim and Roscommon where he himself grew up. But the author of novels including *The Dark* and *Amongst Women* in fact spent much of his life living in Dublin. Having trained as a primary school teacher at St Patrick's College in Drumcondra, he began his career teaching at a school in Clontarf but was fired from his job in the sixties due to clerical disapproval for, among other things, having married in a registry office instead of a church. This experience would inspire his novel *The Leavetaking*.

Though a contemporary of the McDaid's generation of Dublin writers, McGahern didn't see himself as one of them. His Dublin was a private place, made up of cheap seats at the theatres, meeting friends in quiet pubs like the Stag's Head, and reading in the Marino Library at Fairview. In his memoir, he wrote that 'only in Dublin could I disappear into my own and my secret life without being noticed.' When he could no longer teach in Ireland, McGahern moved to London, where he wrote and taught for many years. In the late seventies, he returned to Ireland, buying a farm in the Leitrim countryside of his youth. Though he is seen now as 'Farmer John', as he derisively termed it, McGahern nonetheless maintained links to Dublin, owning what he described as a 'little house' in Stoneybatter, and split his time between city and country. In 2006, following a long period suffering from cancer, he died in Dublin's Mater Hospital.

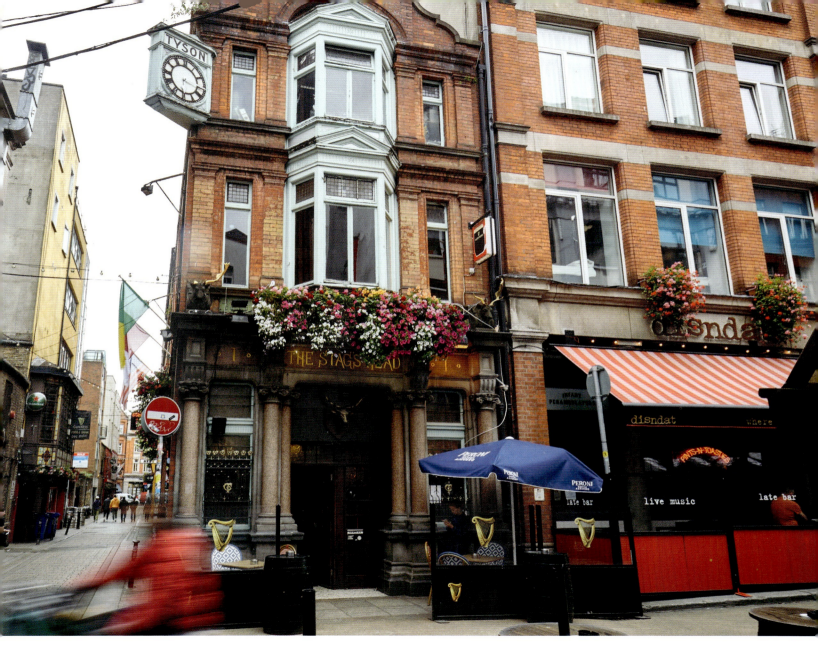

COLM TÓIBÍN

While many of Colm Tóibín's much-loved and prize-winning novels, like *The Blackwater Lightship* and *Brooklyn*, are taken up with the rural Wexford coastline of his youth, Dublin has been an important part of the author's life for many years.

Having moved to the city as a teenager to study at UCD, Tóibín then lived in Barcelona for three years before returning to Dublin in the late seventies. He began a career in journalism, working for local magazines like *In Dublin* that covered city life. His beat included things like the city's nightclub scene and the availability of condoms (not available without a prescription until the mid-eighties). The rhythms of the city were part of his life: Tóibín was sat in the National Library on Kildare Street studying when car bombs planted by the Ulster Volunteer Force went off around the corner on 17 May 1974, before going to Toners pub on Baggot Street to drink and listen to radio news bulletins about the chaos in the city centre through the night. All of these very Dublin experiences would inform Tóibín's fiction writing career, which began with his first novel *The South*, published in 1990. He lives for part of the year in the south Georgian core, near enough to Fitzwilliam Square that he has a resident's key to the private gardens within. As well as fiction and drama, Tóibín writes non-fiction on a wide variety of topics. His papers are archived at the National Library. In 2022 he was announced as the Laureate for Irish Fiction, 2022–4.

LEFT AND ABOVE Tóibín has a key to the residents' garden here.

TOP The writer has known Dublin's Georgian streets since arriving as a student at University College.

TOP Mountjoy Prison, where Behan spent several years in the 1940s.

ABOVE The former Harbour Lights Bar.

RIGHT John Coll's bronze statue of Behan, by the Royal Canal. See page 67 for another of Coll's works.

PAGE 79: The Brendan Behan mural by Shane Sutton on the side of Richmond Cottages in Summerhill.

RIGHT Brendan Behan's grave in Glasnevin Cemetery.

BELOW RIGHT Behan's home on Anglesea Road.

BRENDAN BEHAN

B efore Brendan Behan was a writer, he was a revolutionary. Born into a family of Irish republicans and lovers of literature, Behan's early life in the north inner city in the thirties was marked by the political events of the age. At eight years old he enlisted in Na Fianna, the IRA's youth wing, and in his teens was arrested in Liverpool while in possession of explosives. Three years in an English youth detention centre followed, which he later detailed in his memoir *The Borstal Boy*. Back in Dublin, Behan spent parts of the forties in Mountjoy Prison for his IRA activities. It was here he began to write, with short stories published by Seán Ó'Faoláin's *The Bell* and John Ryan's *Envoy* journal.

After a spell in Paris, where apparently his heavy drinking was not socially accepted, Behan returned to Dublin again and fell in with the crowd of writers associated with McDaid's pub on Harry Street. Those present described him as a great raconteur, a true pub character with a deep well of stories, songs and anecdotes at his fingertips. When not at the bar, he wrote plays and stories, most notably the play *The Quare Fellow*, first staged at the Pike Theatre in 1954. The home Behan shared with his wife, Beatrice, on Anglesea Road in Ballsbridge was the site of many parties and sessions. His alcoholism led to his early decline, however, and Behan described himself as 'a drinker with writing problems.' He collapsed in The Harbour Lights Bar (now Harkin's Harbour Bar/Harkin's) on Echlin Street in 1964, dying at age 41. His impact on later writers and musicians is wide-ranging, with everyone from Shane MacGowan to Morrissey citing him as an influence.

Dublin is a city where there's familiarity without
friendship, loneliness without solitude.

BRENDAN BEHAN

Irish poet (1923-1964)

MAEVE BRENNAN

On a quiet side street in Ranelagh, midway through a pretty row of terraced houses, a plaque sits high on one wall. This plaque marks 48 Cherryfield Avenue, the childhood home of Maeve Brennan. Born in Dublin in 1917, Brennan was the daughter of Irish revolutionaries who took part in the 1916 Easter Rising and went on to have careers in diplomacy that would later bring the family to the US, where Brennan herself eventually became a writer. But first, she spent her childhood here, in this modest terraced house, one that would linger long in her creative imagination.

In New York, where Brennan lived from the forties onwards, she pursued a career in magazines, working as a fashion journalist at *Harper's Bazaar*. She became known for the sophisticated, glamorous figure she cut around town. Here she began writing short fiction, and the first of many short stories, 'The Holy Terror', was published in *Harper's Bazaar* in 1950. Cherryfield Avenue provided the setting for almost half of the short stories Brennan would publish during her career, and her collection *The Springs of Affection* includes many stories of the Derdon family, who live in a home just like the one Brennan herself grew up in Ranelagh.

In addition to her fiction, Brennan wrote a pithy column for the *New Yorker* under the pen name The Long-Winded Lady, which mostly detailed her Manhattan life, the walks she took and characters she met around the city. Like many Irish writers and artists, while she may have made her name abroad, Brennan always kept a firm eye on where she came from. Nevertheless, her work was not published in Ireland during her lifetime. In the years since her death in 1993, Brennan's work has been rediscovered and reappraised by Irish readers and writers, including many woman authors like Anne Enright and Belinda McKeon. The plaque at Cherryfield Avenue, unveiled in 2024, is an important marker of Brennan's impact on her locality, and of its impact on her.

MAEVE BINCHY

Maeve Binchy's death in 2012, aged 73, spurred on an outpouring of memories and stories of the Dalkey author. Beloved for her novels, short stories and journalism, Binchy's work gained her an international readership, as well as many devotees in her hometown of Dublin.

Binchy grew up in Dalkey, describing her childhood there as idyllic. She studied arts at UCD and taught at a girls' school in Ballsbridge before joining the *Irish Times,* where she worked for over 30 years, including as women's editor and as London editor. During this time, she became known as a raconteur and a keen observer of everyday life. In 1973, she claimed in an interview with RTÉ to go to the Pearl bar on Fleet Street, a journalists' hangout, twice a day during her time at the paper.

Binchy began writing and publishing fiction in her thirties and would go on to publish seventeen novels, mostly about the lives of Irish women and men. Many capture the particular social nuances of life in Dublin, including the short story collection *Dublin 4* and *Quentins*, set at a fictional restaurant in the city. 'I know the feel of Dublin very well,' she said in a 2010 interview. 'Every part has its own character.'

After a time living in London, Binchy and her husband, Gordon Snell, moved back to Dalkey in the eighties. Binchy's love of Dublin life knew no bounds. In 2011, she and her husband Gordon made a cameo appearance in the popular Dublin soap opera *Fair City,* where they played restaurant diners. After her death in 2012, her hometown of Dalkey named a mosaic-decorated memorial garden in her honour at the local library, where readers can sit on a bench and remember Binchy and her work.

OPPOSITE Dalkey village, with Dalkey Castle (below).

ABOVE Mosaic artwork in the memorial garden to Maeve Binchy in Dalkey.

THIS PAGE The peaceful Grand Canal, just across the street from Bowen's childhood home.

ELIZABETH BOWEN

The daughter of a barrister and a member of a prominent Anglo-Irish family, Elizabeth Bowen was born in 1899 at 15 Herbert Place, in a Georgian townhouse facing directly onto the Grand Canal. During Bowen's childhood, her family divided the year between this house and the family seat of Bowen's Court in Co. Cork, which she would later inherit. The Dublin of her youth was to her mind the centre of the universe, and undeniably a small and privileged place – in her memoir *Seven Winters*, she writes of her mother not knowing how to get her daughter to a dancing exhibition in nearby Rathmines.

Though she lived most of her life in England, Bowen's novels of the Protestant Ascendency became symbolic of the decline of a particular era of Irish life. As the influence of the landed Anglo-Irish gentry began to wane in the first decades of the twentieth century, Bowen's work formed an elegy for her people, best typified in the novel *The Last September*. Set during the War of Independence at a country house, that bears close similarities with Bowen's Court, *The Last September* brings to life the violence and destruction of that era. Later, during the Second World War, Bowen wrote espionage reports on Ireland for the British Ministry of Information. She did not return to live in Dublin during her lifetime but did live for a period at Bowen's Court, where she entertained Irish and international artists and writers until forced to sell the house in 1959. It was bought by a developer and quickly demolished.

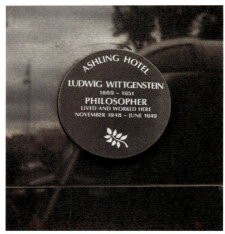

LEFT AND BELOW The former
Ross's Hotel on Parkgate Street,
Wittgenstein's first home in Dublin.

LUDWIG WITTGENSTEIN

During the Second World War, the Viennese philosopher Ludwig Wittgenstein began to feel disillusioned about his position as chair of philosophy at Cambridge. By 1947, he was at the end of his tether and quit his professorship to focus instead on his writing. His first stop after Cambridge was Dublin, drawn to the city through his friendship with a former student turned psychiatrist named Con Drury, who lived and worked there. Wittgenstein took rooms at Ross's Hotel, now the Ashling Hotel, on Parkgate Street, where a plaque honours the time he spent living and working there during 1948 and 1949. The philosopher seemed to enjoy life in Dublin, regularly taking lunch at Bewley's Café – always a plain omelette and a cup of coffee – as well as walking in the Zoological Gardens in Phoenix Park and sitting in quiet contemplation in the Botanic Gardens in Glasnevin. On one occasion, he and Drury bought disposable cameras and climbed to the top of Nelson's Pillar on O'Connell Street to photograph the city.

During his time in Dublin, he wrote texts that would become part of his landmark work, *Philosophical Investigations*. But Wittgenstein would not live to see this book completed and published. After leaving Dublin in 1949, he was diagnosed with cancer and saw out his final days back in Cambridge. His Dublin friend Drury came to his bedside shortly before the great philosopher passed in 1951.

THIS PAGE The Botanic Gardens in Glasnevin, one of the writer's favourite spots. He liked to spend time writing here, and is remembered with a plaque on his favourite set of steps.

EDNA O'BRIEN

While the novelist Edna O'Brien only lived in Dublin briefly, it was a formative experience that left a lasting mark in her work. Moving to the city from Clare in the late forties, she spent four years living in digs near Phoenix Park and working in a chemist on the Cabra Road. She cycled around the city attending lectures in the evenings as she trained to be a pharmacist, once spotting the revolutionary and object of W.B. Yeats's affections, Maud Gonne, addressing a crowd on Baggot Street. O'Brien was keen to experience what Dublin, and life, had to offer an ambitious young woman: ballrooms, theatres, romance, and proximity to the many ghosts of Ireland's literary past.

All of this would feed into her first novel, *The Country Girls*, about two friends Kate and Baba and their transition from the world of girlhood into adult life. The book was banned by the Irish censorship board on publication in 1960 for its broaching of sexual matters, with the Minister for Justice describing it as filth that had no place in an Irish home. Copies were burned around the country, including in O'Brien's hometown. By this time, O'Brien had married Ernest Gébler and left Dublin for London, where she would live for most of her life. But Dublin remains enamoured with her today – and keen to atone for the way she and her books were treated over the years. In 2019, *The Country Girls Trilogy* was chosen for Dublin City Libraries' 'One Dublin, One Book' initiative, with readers all over the city invited to follow Kate and Baba through O'Brien's three pivotal novels of Irish womanhood.

OPPOSITE LEFT The Cabra Road shops, where O'Brien worked.

OPPOSITE RIGHT O'Brien lived near Phoenix Park for four years.

ABOVE The tea rooms at Phoenix Park.

LEFT The Wellington Monument, the tallest obelisk in Europe and situated in the park.

PAGE 90: The beauty of Phoenix Park.

The truth is that I am in love with Dublin.
I think it is the most beautiful town that I have
ever seen, mountains at the back and the sea in
front, and long roads winding through decaying
suburbs and beautiful woods.

GEORGE A. MOORE

Irish novelist, short-story writer, poet, art critic, memoirist and dramatist (1852-1933)

MARY LAVIN

Born in the US to Irish parents in 1912, Mary Lavin grew up in County Meath, having returned with her family in 1925. She moved to Dublin as a teenager to attend Loreto College, St Stephen's Green. Next came a degree at UCD, and soon Lavin began writing short stories about rural Ireland. Her first collection, *Tales from Bective Bridge*, was published in 1942.

Marriage and motherhood soon followed, and Lavin put down her pen for some time. But after the death of her husband William Walsh in 1954, the financial pressure of running a household and raising three daughters alone brought Lavin back to writing short stories. The writer JD Salinger introduced Lavin to an editor at the *New Yorker*, sounding the starting gun of a long-running publishing relationship. The magazine published sixteen of Lavin's stories across eighteen years, and the writer would buy her Dublin home, a mews house at 11 Lad Lane near the Grand Canal, with her first *New Yorker* cheque.

Rarely has Dublin known a literary salon like the Lavin house on Lad Lane. This home became a drop-in centre for passing friends, thanks in part to her hospitality and good humour. This social circle included many prominent writers: legend has it that Patrick Kavanagh fell asleep on the sofa. Frank O'Connor, a neighbour and fellow Irish writer published by the *New Yorker*, would drop by, as would Eavan Boland, Seán Ó'Faoláin and Elizabeth Bowen. The Lavin parties became notorious. In the sixties, Dublin's pubs were still not always welcoming places for women, and it's easy to see why someone as charismatic as Lavin might prefer to entertain at home. Her granddaughter, the author Kathleen MacMahon, later quoted Lavin as saying that she 'made too much soup for too many people', but clearly her guests were happy in her home. One guest was a young John McGahern, who wrote a note to Lavin thanking her after the fact. It was, he admitted, only the second party he had ever attended.

ABOVE AND LEFT Wilton Park.

TOP Lavin's mews house at Lad Lane.

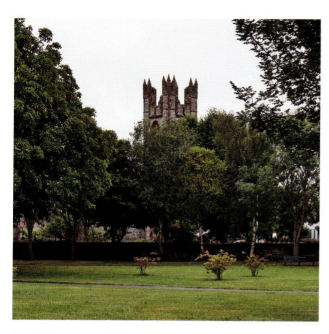

Corrán Marino
Áit Bhreithe

Abraham 'Bram' Stoker
(1847 - 1912)

Údar an Úrscéil Ghotaigh Cháiliúil
'DRACULA'

Marino Crescent
Birthplace of

Abraham 'Bram' Stoker
(1847 - 1912)

Author of the Famous Novel
'DRACULA'

Comhairle Cathrach
Bhaile Átha Cliath
Dublin City Council

TOP AND ABOVE Bram Stoker Park,
renamed after the neighbourhood's
most famous resident.

BRAM STOKER

The picturesque curve of Marino Crescent in Clontarf holds two notable distinctions: It is one of the only Georgian crescents in Ireland, and it's also home to the birthplace of Bram Stoker. The author of *Dracula* was born here at 15 Marino Crescent in 1847, and the adjacent park is now named in his honour.

Stoker's youth in Dublin had a long-lasting impact on him. While studying at Trinity College, he played many sports and presided over both of the university's two debating societies. This is where his early interest in theatre emerged, something that would come to dictate the shape of his life and work. After university, Stoker worked as a courts' inspector in the civil service, reviewing plays for the *Dublin Evening Mail* in his free time. He was friends with Jane Wilde, mother of Oscar Wilde and noted folklorist, and the vampire at the heart of his most famous novel would show the influence of her ideas on Irish legends and superstitions.

Stoker moved to London in 1878 to work in theatre and pursue his writing career, but traces of his Irish origins worked their way into many of his novels, including *The Snake's Pass* and *Dracula*. Some modern academics view the character of Dracula as a stand-in for English absentee landlords, who were blamed for poor management of their tenancies during the Great Famine. Stoker died in London in 1912, and today Dublin celebrates his Irish legacy with an annual arts festival – timed, of course, to coincide with Halloween.

FLANN O'BRIEN

Flann O'Brien was born Brian O'Nolan in 1911 and was the third in a family of twelve children. The O'Nolan family lived for a time on Herbert Place, and Brian was educated at the Christian Brothers school on Synge Street and at Blackrock College. As a writer, he used a variety of pen names in his career, creating authorial personas that changed depending on his output. 'Flann O'Brien' became the most prominent of these names, using it to publish his novel *At Swim-Two-Birds*. This novel, marked by its satirical humour and use of early postmodernism, made Flann O'Brien's name in the Dublin literary scene that coalesced around pubs like the Palace and McDaid's.

But unlike some of those writers he socialized with, O'Nolan had other demands on his time. The death of his father during O'Nolan's mid-twenties left him as the family breadwinner, so he worked all his life as a civil servant. Writing took place around this job, which also created the need for pseudonyms, since those who worked in the civil service were meant to be apolitical. As 'Myles

RIGHT 10 Belmont Avenue in Donnybrook, where O'Nolan lived while making his living as a writer.

BELOW Herbert Place, where the O'Nolan family lived.

na Gopaleen', O'Nolan wrote columns for the *Irish Times* from the forties to the sixties. Within these satirical columns, it was open season: anyone could fall victim to his mocking eye, including his government colleagues, and his drinking buddies and fellow writers. When it became clear that O'Nolan the civil servant was the same person as na Gopaleen, the acerbic and troublesome newspaper columnist, he was made to retire from his job. His hand had finally been forced, after years of walking the tightrope between respectability and radicalism.

In later life, O'Nolan lived in Donnybrook and Ballsbridge. As the novelist Flann O'Brien, he was mostly dissatisfied and disappointed by what he perceived as the failure of his career. At the time of his death in 1966, *The Third Policeman* was still unpublished, having been rejected by several publishers to O'Nolan's dismay. It was finally published posthumously in 1967, some twenty-seven years after O'Nolan had completed it. Today it is widely regarded as a classic of Irish literature.

SAMUEL BECKETT

Born in Foxrock, County Dublin in 1906, Samuel Beckett's relationship with his hometown was not a simple one. After studying English, Italian and French at Trinity College, Beckett lived above his father's quantity surveying firm on Clare Street, where he wrote his first novel *More Pricks Than Kicks*. He soon moved to Paris and would live in France for much of his life. In Paris in the thirties, he met another of Dublin's literary exiles – James Joyce. Their friendship grew from time spent in the city's cafés, and Beckett helped Joyce with typing parts of *Finnegans Wake*.

But compared to Joyce's output, Beckett did not allow Dublin to loom so large in his work. His writing made him a literary celebrity around the world, but his relationship with home and family was vexed. Nonetheless, the city had much to offer him throughout his life. Visits to the National Gallery gave him a chance to steep himself in art and art history. In fact it was his friend, the poet Thomas MacGreevy who would later become director of the Gallery, who introduced him to Joyce in Paris.

Beckett could never quite free himself from the bonds his hometown held over him. Called back to Ireland as a witness in the libel trial of writer Oliver St John Gogarty in 1937, he was derided in court as a 'bawd and blasphemer' from Paris.

OPPOSITE AND LEFT Beckett wrote his first novel here on Clare Street, where his father's business premises were located. Beckett lived upstairs.

The insult stung, and Beckett vowed never to live in Ireland again. The first full English-language production of his play *Waiting for Godot* was staged at the avant-garde (and now defunct) Pike Theatre in 1955, accompanied by a warning from the producers in the *Irish Times* that the play would contain 'crudities' of language, and 'lady guests' in particular may be offended.

Life abroad suited Beckett much better, though he did accept an honorary doctorate from Trinity in 1959, and became the first Saoi of Aosdána, the highest honour available in the Irish arts. Shortly before his death in 1989, Beckett wrote to Dublin's Lord Mayor, noting with pleasure 'the growth of interest in my work among the younger generation of my countrymen'.

Two years after his death, the Gate Theatre (see page 40) in conjunction with Trinity College and RTÉ, the national broadcaster, staged all nineteen of Beckett's plays in a landmark festival. The huge production later toured to London and New York. *The New York Times* labelled it 'the dramatic equivalent of a museum retrospective of a major artist'. Today, Beckett's legacy at home is written into the city's fabric, with theatres, bridges and even a naval vessel named after this great Dublin writer.

JOHN BANVILLE

John Banville's first memories of Dublin came in the form of birthday trips from his childhood home in Wexford. His birthday fell on 8 December, traditionally the day that country-dwellers visit the capital for Christmas shopping, and his mother would take him on the train. Later, he would make the city his own, moving in the early sixties to Upper Mount Street, to share a second-floor flat with his aunt. Here, his downstairs neighbour was Anne Yeats, the artist daughter of W.B. Yeats.

The Georgian quarter had a lasting influence on the young Banville. In his memoir of a life in Dublin, *Time Pieces*, he details life on the fringes of Baggotonia. But the city's mid-century bohemian squalor, along with its boozy writers, weren't quite right for him. He described McDaid's pub as a place 'where many a masterpiece was talked into thin air and spirited away by the fumes of alcohol.' Banville preferred Ryan's of Parkgate Street, a charming Victorian pub by Phoenix Park. He worked as sub-editor at the *Irish Press* and later the *Irish Times*, where he also held the role of literary editor.

Later in his career, after much success for his literary novels (including the Booker Prize-winning *The Sea*), Banville would revisit the Georgian Dublin of his youth in his writing. In his crime novels published under the pen name Benjamin Black, his protagonist Quirke, a pathologist in fifties Dublin, lives at Banville's own former flat on Mount Street, passing through the same Georgian streets his creator walked as a young man.

OPPOSITE ABOVE St Stephen's, known as the Pepper Canister Church, on Upper Mount Street.

OPPOSITE BELOW Banville lived with his aunt on the street.

ABOVE Ryan's on Parkgate Street, a favourite pub near Phoenix Park.

PLA

CES

ABOVE The Four Courts, on the banks of the Liffey.

OPPOSITE ABOVE The Samuel Beckett Bridge.

OPPOSITE CENTRE A view of O'Connell Bridge crossing the Liffey.

OPPOSITE BELOW The Sean O'Casey Bridge.

PAGE 106: The James Joyce Bridge.

RIVER LIFFEY

There is little so permanent in the fabric of a city than its main river. The Liffey, which runs through the centre of Dublin and cleaves Dublin into Northside and Southside, has always been a source of inspiration and a place to reflect for the writers who have lived here.

Often represented in folklore and literature as Anna Liffey or Anna Livia, the female embodiment of the river, the Liffey has had a captivating effect on many Irish authors. James Joyce's notoriously difficult novel *Finnegans Wake* opens with a description of the river, and much of the novel is taken up with it through the voice of the 'river-woman' Anna Livia Plurabelle. In 'An Encounter', a story from Joyce's *Dubliners,* two boys play truant from school and take a ferry across the river on their way to the seafront. In *Under the Net*, Iris Murdoch comments on the filth of the Liffey, while Eavan Boland wrote of the river as an Irish woman, tracing her life through the land and the city of Dublin in the poem 'Anna Liffey'.

Part of its enduring allure has to do with the way the city falls around the River Liffey, with many important buildings and forms of industry taking place in its wake. Among these are the Four Courts, the centre of Ireland's justice system, which has been located at Inns Quay since the late eighteenth century. Colm Tóibín's novel The Heather Blazing opens with the fictional judge Eamon Redmond gazing out at the river from his office with the courts.

The hold that the river has over the city's authors has been recognized more recently in the naming of three of the Liffey's newest bridges. James Joyce, Samuel Beckett and Sean O'Casey all lend their names to bridges that span the river; grand architectural designs that connect the two sides of the city, and that bring Dubliners closer to the enigmatic and everlasting river itself.

In Dublin's fair city, where the girls are so pretty,
I first set my eyes on sweet Molly Malone.
She pushed her wheelbarrow
Through streets broad and narrow
Crying, 'Cockles and mussels! Alive, alive-oh!'

TRADITIONAL BALLAD

TRINITY COLLEGE DUBLIN

The picturesque walled campus of Trinity College appears in the heart of Dublin like a small city within a city. As much a draw for history-loving tourists as for students themselves, the college contains a great deal of the city's broader intellectual lineage. Elegant buildings arranged in quadrangles around greens and cobblestones have been home to many of Ireland's great writers over the years during their studies, including Samuel Beckett, Bram Stoker, J.M. Synge and Jonathan Swift.

Countless other writers have passed through Trinity as students or as lecturers themselves. Named for another of its famous alumna, the university's Oscar Wilde Centre for Irish Writing is a major hub for literary studies and often hosts international authors as visiting creative writing teachers. The American author Richard Ford taught at Trinity for several years, and Irish writers including John McGahern, Sebastian Barry and the playwright Marina Carr have held the Writer

ABOVE Front Square, as seen on the BBC's 2020 adaptation of *Normal People*.

LEFT AND FAR LEFT The New Library.

TOP The School of Botany.

ABOVE The Old Library's Long Room –
the exterior hiding the treasures within.

LEFT The Old Library.

RIGHT AND BELOW The Old Library's Long Room, lined with leather-bound books and home to the Book of Kells.

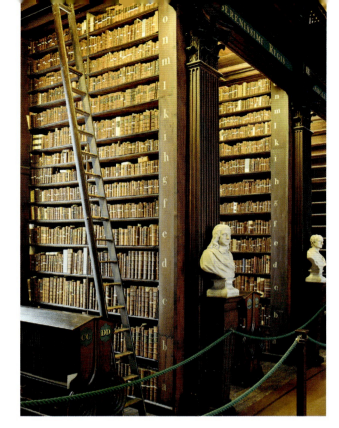

Fellowship at the university. *Icarus*, a student-run literary journal, has been publishing work by current students, alumni and staff since 1950, and has featured poetry from Eavan Boland, Simon Armitage and Paul Muldoon.

The eighteenth-century Old Library, with its central Long Room chamber, is possibly the Platonic ideal of what a hallowed university library should look like. Floor-to-ceiling bookshelves spanning two floors house 200,000 of the college's oldest books. Students don't usually study here, but visitors can take a tour and see many of the rare manuscripts in the collection, including the illuminated *Book of Kells*, a stunningly intricate ninth-century gospel.

Fans of contemporary Irish writing will recognize Trinity's campus as the setting for Sally Rooney's novels *Conversations with Friends* and *Normal People*. *Normal People*'s TV adaptation was shot on location in Trinity, bringing Front Square and Botany Bay to a generation of readers. Rooney herself studied English at Trinity and was elected Scholar in 2011.

BAGGOT STREET

Baggotonia, as the area around Baggot Street Bridge has long been nicknamed, is more a state of mind than a neighbourhood. For many Dubliners, the name will conjure up smoky images of mid-century bohemian lifestyles, boozy afternoons in the company of poets-slash-civil-servants and at least one member of a band like The Dubliners. Spanning the area from Merrion Row with its government buildings on one side to Pembroke Road in leafy Ballsbridge, from the forties onwards Baggotonia came to represent a neighbourhood of Georgian terraces where elegant embassies sit alongside squalid bedsits.

The availability of cheap rooms close to the city centre meant that during the Forties, the area began to draw a bohemian crowd looking for a place of their own. Soon it became the epicentre of a literary and cultural scene including the likes of Brendan Behan, Patrick Kavanagh and Flann O'Brien, as well as many other artists and writers in their orbit. Many would write about the area and its village-like charms in their work. Later, others passed through, including the painter Lucian Freud, who rented a room in the area in the late forties.

At that time, The Catacombs nightclub on Fitzwilliam Place was a popular drinking den for Baggotonians, and according to Behan, it was a place where anything went, including debates, romance and fights. During the day, Parsons Bookshop on Baggot Street was a literary institution for local writers. Today, Parsons is an insurance office and Baggot Street is quieter and more sanitized than in its romantic bohemian heyday. But many still sense the ghostly presence of its artistic forefathers on the neighbourhood's leafy street corners.

THIS PAGE Contrasting architectural styles along the street.

LEFT The Baggot Street Bridge over the Grand Canal.

LEFT 41 Brighton Square, Joyce's Rathgar birthplace.

BELOW Rathgar, Dublin 6.

RATHMINES AND RATHGAR

Perhaps the greatest claim the leafy suburb of Rathgar can make is that in 1882, James Joyce was born here. 41 Brighton Square, a pretty red-brick terraced house, was home to Joyce and his family until 1884 when they moved across the neighbourhood to Castlewood Avenue in Rathmines. But both Rathmines and Rathgar have a robust literary and artistic character that extends far beyond Joyce himself.

With its large houses and long history of affluent middle and upper-class residents, many famous names have called the Dublin 6 postcode home. W.B. Yeats spent part of his childhood in the area, and George William Russell, another key figure in the Irish Literary Revival, lived at 17 Rathgar Avenue. Russell, a poet, critic and editor who wrote under the pseudonym Æ, held regular gatherings of artists and writers in his home, fostering a culture of ideas that brought people together. After his death in Bournemouth in 1935, his body was returned to Dublin and buried in nearby Mount Jerome cemetery. The graveside oration was delivered by the short story writer Frank O'Connor, who described Æ as 'the father to three generations of Irish writers'.

During the twentieth century, Georgian and Victorian houses around Dublin 6 were often divvied up into clusters of bedsits, earning the area the nickname Flatland. Rathmines especially was the first port of call for many students moving to Dublin for university. Today, the Rathmines Library is a centre for literary activity in the area, and the Rathmines Writers' Workshop has been meeting regularly since 1990.

ABOVE The clock tower on Rathmines Town Hall.

LEFT Rathmines Library.

RIGHT The Yeats memorial bronze by Henry Moore.

OPPOSITE LEFT The Grafton Street entrance, through the 1907 Fusiliers' Arch.

ST STEPHEN'S GREEN

With twenty-seven acres of Victorian parkland in the centre of Southside Dublin, St Stephen's Green has provided a public place of peace and quiet for Dubliners for almost 150 years. In *A Portrait of the Artist as a Young Man*, Stephen Dedalus calls the park 'my green', and with James Joyce studying in the adjacent Newman House, one assumes the author himself felt similarly to his literary alter ego. A bust of Joyce is placed on the south side of the park, facing his alma mater and with Dedalus's possessive quote etched on the pillar. Closer to the park's centre, a bronze Henry Moore sculpture sits at the centre of the W.B. Yeats Memorial, surrounded by stone terraces that form a loose amphitheatre fit for a poet's oration.

But the park is more than a memorial to Irish figures of the past. It has also been the site of important historical events. During the first days of the Easter Rising, St Stephen's Green was a battleground. Trenches were dug by the Irish Citizen Army and machine guns fired by the British Army from the nearby Shelbourne Hotel, causing the rebels to retreat. The casualties in St Stephen's Green included several birds and waterfowl, giving rise to the poet Paula Meehan's memorably-titled sonnet, 'Them Ducks Died for Ireland'.

W.B. YEATS 1865-1939
A TRIBUTE IN BRONZE BY
HENRY MOORE, ERECTED
BY ADMIRERS OF THE POET
OCTOBER 1967

OPPOSITE RIGHT ABOVE The bust of Joyce, which incorporates a quote commemorating Stephen Dedalus.

OPPOSITE RIGHT BELOW The peaceful St Stephen's Green pond.

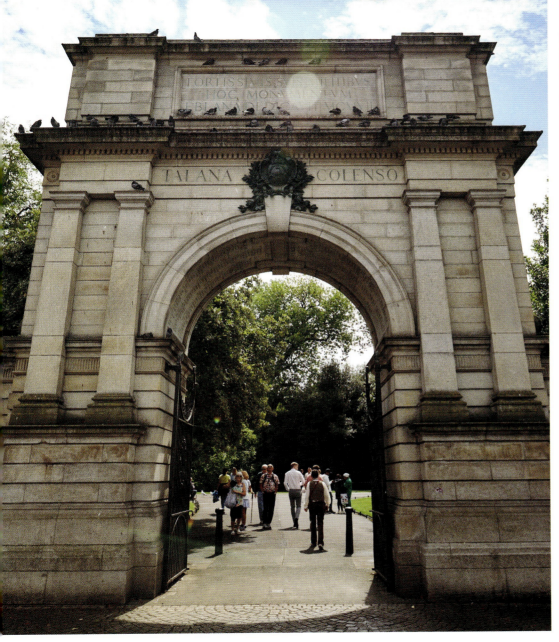

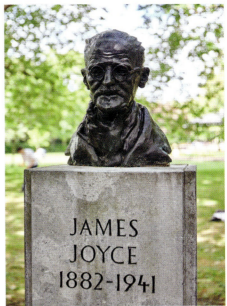

JAMES
JOYCE
1882-1941

TOP AND ABOVE Terraced Georgian houses in Mountjoy Square and its park.

RIGHT Croke Park stadium looms over redbrick cottages.

SUMMERHILL

In the shadow of Croke Park, Ireland's largest sports stadium, this inner-city neighbourhood has been home to some of the city's greatest writers. The O'Connell School on North Richmond Street educated the poet Thomas Kinsella and is mentioned in 'Araby', from James Joyce's *Dubliners*. Brendan Behan (see page 76) grew up first in the tenements of Mountjoy Square before his family was encouraged to move out to the suburb of Crumlin, which he and his brothers referred to as 'Siberia'. He is remembered with a large mural on a gable wall in Richmond Cottages, complete with pint of stout and stack of books. Many pubs and newsagents in the area will claim to have been Behan's preferred local, or the place he purchased his cigarettes, but considering the author spent much of his life in prison or in Crumlin, it's likely that these claims are no more than Behanesque bravado.

More recently, Roddy Doyle, the Booker Prize-winning author, founded Fighting Words, a writing workshop for children and young people, with Sean Love in 2009. Its headquarters on Behan Square is a hub for local young people looking for an introduction to creative writing, ensuring that the spark of literature in the north inner city is kept aflame for a new generation.

PEARSE STREET AND WESTLAND ROW

For many Irish people outside the capital, Westland Row could be considered the gateway to the city. The train station here, formerly known as Westland Row and today as Pearse Station, was the starting point for those arriving to the city from the south-east of the country. Among them: John Banville, who wrote lyrically in his memoir *Time Pieces* about walking up the street as a child on annual shopping trips from Wexford with his mother.

Pearse Street, formerly Great Brunswick Street, runs perpendicular to Westland Row and east from Trinity College towards Dublin Bay and also holds a wealth of literary history. James Joyce sang at the Antient Concert Rooms on Pearse Street in 1904 and also used the venue as a setting for his story 'A Mother' from *Dubliners*. This building later became a cinema and today is used as offices. In *Ulysses*, Leopold Bloom wanders up Westland Row on his way to purchase soap at Sweny's (see page 134). He collects a love letter from his mistress in the street's post office, then ducks into St Andrew's Church, taking in his surroundings while losing himself in various trains of thought.

Further east sits the Dublin City Library and Archive, in a handsome sandstone building, purpose-built in 1907. Inside, readers can consult extensive collections of literary and cultural history – watched over by the severed head of a statue of Viscount Horatio Nelson. Previously standing atop a tall pillar on O'Connell Street, both statue and pillar were blown up by the IRA in 1966. The head, which remained mostly intact, was then purloined by art students from the National College of Art and Design who brought it on a madcap six-month tour of Ireland and the UK, before handing it back to Dublin Corporation.

OPPOSITE LEFT St Andrew's church.

OPPOSITE RIGHT Pearse Station on Westland Row.

ABOVE Dublin City Library on Pearse Street.

THE IRISH TIMES, TARA STREET

Ireland's newspaper of record does more than simply report the news. It also acts as an incubator of sorts for Irish literary talent. Many of Ireland's pre-eminent poets have had their work published by the *Irish Times*, including Paul Muldoon, Eavan Boland, Thomas Kinsella, Seamus Heaney and Eiléan Ní Chuilleanáin. Numerous Irish authors of note have also passed through the *Irish Times* as employees. The offices of the paper, which were located on D'Olier Street for over a century, were frequented by novelists John Banville, who worked as sub-editor and literary editor during the eighties and nineties, and Maeve Binchy (see page 82), a former columnist who also held the roles of London editor and women's editor at the paper. She was sceptical about her suitability for the latter role, later saying she knew nothing about either fashion or cooking.

In 2006, the *Irish Times* moved from D'Olier Street to its current premises on Tara Street, where literature still sits alongside news journalism. After the death of Sinéad O'Connor in 2023, the paper devoted its front page to 'A Blackbird in Dun Laoghaire', a commemorative poem written by her brother, the writer Joseph O'Connor.

ABOVE AND RIGHT The paper's current home on Tara Street.

ABOVE The nineteenth-century clock has moved with the newspaper to various premises, and is now at home on Tara Street.

RIGHT Bustling Manor Street in Stoneybatter.

BELOW A stone marker on Manor Street where Stoneybatter begins.

STONEYBATTER

Just up the Liffey from the bustle of the city centre, Stoneybatter is a historic neighbourhood that has become a hub of cultural activity in its own right. Residents of the quiet cottage-lined streets behind the main thoroughfare have included novelists Colm Tóibín and John McGahern in the past, and writers and artists continue to live and socialize in the charismatic inner suburb.

At its heart is The Lilliput Press, an independent publisher and bookshop hidden away on Sitric Road, one of many streets named in tribute to the former Viking suburb's history. Sharing a name with the fictional island in Jonathan Swift's *Gulliver's Travels*, the press keeps contemporary and classic authors in print, while around it, the motley array of pubs and cafés play host to modern bohemian life.

Bounded to the south by the river, to the north by the North Circular Road and to the west by the vast, verdant Phoenix Park, it retains a distinctive neighbourhood feel despite its proximity to the centre of Dublin. The nearby Cobblestone pub in Smithfield has an international reputation as a venue for Irish traditional music, and describes itself as a 'drinking pub with a music problem'. Attendees can sit or stand with friends in the classic wood-lined bar sipping a Guinness at their leisure as singers, fiddlers, concertina players and others entertain the room from the window booth. But be warned: the bar staff have been known to shush chatterboxes during the more delicate numbers.

THIS PAGE The Lilliput Press, one of Ireland's leading independent publishers, has a bookshop and offices in Stoneybatter.

JAMES JOYCE'S

DUBLIN

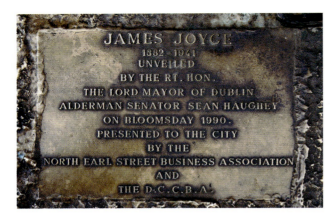

TOP AND ABOVE The James Joyce statue on Grafton Street was unveiled in 1990.

JAMES JOYCE

Perhaps no writer has done as much for their hometown through their work as James Joyce. For many literary visitors to Dublin, it is Joyce's writing, so much of and about the city, that draws them here. Born in Rathgar on 2 February 1882, Joyce was the eldest of ten children. The family moved around the city during his childhood, giving the young Joyce a glimpse of many different versions of Dublin. But the city would not be his home forever. Shortly after graduating from UCD in 1902, he met his future wife, Nora Barnacle, and the pair moved to mainland Europe. Joyce would spend the rest of his life living in France, Switzerland, Austria and Italy.

Nonetheless, Dublin is everywhere in Joyce's work. From the visions of everyday urban life in *Dubliners* to the spirit of the River Liffey running through *Finnegans Wake*, the city's multifaceted, sometimes chaotic nature is present on every page of Joyce's writing. For this reason, Dublin is something of a site of pilgrimage for readers of Joyce from all over the world. Every year on 16 June, the day commemorated in *Ulysses*, the city turns into a living recreation of Leopold Bloom and Stephen Dedalus's world. Bloomsday, first celebrated by the writers Patrick Kavanagh and Anthony Cronin in 1954, has become a magnet for Joyce's modern-day readers, who don their straw boaters and take to the streets to retrace Bloom's own footsteps for a day. It's hard to know what the author would have made of it all from his vantage point overseas, but the exchange he made with the city is clear today. Dublin gave James Joyce his subject matter, and James Joyce gave the city its literary reputation in return.

... he gazed southward over the bay,
empty save for the smokeplume of the
mailboat vague on the bright skyline,
and a sail tacking by the Muglins.

ULYSSES

THIS TREE WAS PLANTED BY COUNCILLOR W.C. WILLOUGHBY
AN CATHAOIRLEACH CORPORATION OF DUN LAOGHAIRE
ON 18TH MAY, 1963, TO MARK THE CENTENARY
OF THE BIRTH OF JAMES JOYCE.

TOP An easier way into the water
via the beach at Sandycove.

BOTTOM An inscribed rock looking
outover Dublin Bay,

SANDYCOVE

From the opening lines of James Joyce's *Ulysses*, the reader is thrown into the middle of things: Joycean Dublin in all its glory, viewed from the rooftop of a Martello tower on the coast. The decommissioned military tower in the pretty seaside suburb of Sandycove is the home of Buck Mulligan and on the morning of 16 June 1904, he and Stephen Dedalus talk there on its parapets, looking out at the 'snotgreen sea' of Dublin Bay before them. In the pages that follow, Stephen follows Mulligan down to the Forty Foot – still a beloved spot for Dublin's sea swimmers today – and they take to the water. It's a memorable moment in Irish literature, and every year on Bloomsday, contemporary Joyceans follow in Stephen and Mulligan's footsteps, beginning their day with a bracing dip in the sea at Sandycove.

FINN'S HOTEL

1 South Leinster Street, Dublin 2

On 10 June 1904, Joyce was walking near Trinity College when he spotted Nora Barnacle, chambermaid, leaving Finn's Hotel, where she lived and worked in central Dublin. Six days later, Joyce and Nora would go out together for the first time, beginning a relationship that would continue until the author's death in 1941.

The couple came from two very different worlds – Barnacle was born into poverty, in a Galway workhouse, while Joyce had had a solidly middle-class Dublin Jesuit upbringing in the suburbs. For Barnacle, it was not exactly love at first sight. On meeting Joyce, she initially saw him for what he was – just another Dublin lad who seemed to be trying it on with a girl from the country. But over time, their relationship became passionate and loving, and the two left Dublin for the continent later that same year.

Joyce immortalized the fateful date of their meeting in *Ulysses*, which takes place entirely on the date of the couple's first outing together – 16 June 1904. Finn's Hotel has long since closed, but the Lincoln's Inn pub, housed in the same building, claims that its front door was the original hotel entrance. Look up from South Leinster Street and you'll see the 'ghost sign' of Finn's Hotel still visible on the building's red-brick gable wall.

15 USHER'S ISLAND

A typical Georgian townhouse located overlooking the Liffey, 15 Usher's Island is a living piece of literary history. At the end of the nineteenth century, this house was home to James Joyce's grand-aunts, who also ran a music school inside. Their home became the setting for 'The Dead', one of the most beloved stories from Joyce's *Dubliners*. 'The Dead' takes place at a Christmas party inside 15 Usher's Island, with Gabriel Conroy and his wife Gretta attending the annual dinner at the home of his aunts. Political discussion and songs ensue, and when it comes time to leave, Gabriel finds his wife Gretta lost in reverie on the staircase. A song she has heard at the party has reminded her of her youth. 'The Dead' turned this address into a literary landmark, but over the years it has been occupied by squatters or left vacant.

The director John Huston used the building's exterior for his film adaptation of 'The Dead' in 1987. For many Dubliners, the house is a surviving piece of Joyce's Dublin. When plans were made to turn the building into a tourist hostel, Colm Tóibín and others filed an appeal against the decision on the grounds of cultural heritage, but sadly this didn't succeed. Whatever happens to 15 Usher's Island, the legacy of 'The Dead' is nonetheless written into the city's geography here. The house faces a bridge named in Joyce's honour, connecting Usher's Island to Blackhall Place on the north of the river, which was opened on Bloomsday in 2003.

TOP The shopfront with original signage ('Chemist – Druggist') above the door.

ABOVE The store caters for those on a Joycean pilgrimage around Dublin.

RIGHT Lincoln Place in central Dublin.

RIGHT AND BELOW Vintage articles on display that could date from Joyce's day. And is that lemon soap on the bottom shelf?

SWENY'S

1 Lincoln Place, Dublin 2

It's mid-morning on 16 June 1904, and Leopold Bloom has things to do and places to be. On his list: Order some lotion for his wife, Molly Bloom, at Sweny's pharmacy on Lincoln Place. He does so, and throws in some lemon soap for good measure, then continues about his business. It's a small incident in the span of *Ulysses*, but no harm: it's enough to make Sweny's pharmacy a landmark destination on any whistle-stop tour of Joycean Dublin. Sweny's is still open today, claiming to be 'preserved through neglect' and thus broadly similar to how it was in 1904 when Bloom pushed open the front door. Nowadays, it's less of a pharmacy, having stopped filling prescriptions in 2009, and more of a one-stop shop for all things *Ulysses*. Inside, you'll find space for hosting reading groups and tours, as well as selling copies of Joyce's novels, straw boater hats and, of course, that famous lemon soap.

ABOVE The village proudly declares its associations with Joyce and *Finnegans Wake* in particular.

OPPOSITE Mullingar House is still going strong in Chapelizod.

CHAPELIZOD

A peaceful country village on the fringes of the city, Chapelizod is unlike any other neighbourhood in Dublin. It also holds its share of Joycean history. In the *Dubliners* story 'A Painful Case', Chapelizod is home to Mr James Duffy, a bank cashier who chose the neighbourhood 'because he wished to live as far as possible from the city of which he was a citizen and because he found all the other suburbs of Dublin mean, modern and pretentious'.

But it is in *Finnegans Wake* that Joyce is most concerned with Chapelizod. The village sits on the banks of the River Liffey, and it is perhaps for this reason that Joyce chose it as the home of Humphrey Chimpden Earwicker and his wife Anna Livia Plurabelle, the novel's main characters, if such things can be said to exist. The local pub, the Mullingar House, is central to the novel and Earwicker is described as the pub's owner. Today a plaque hangs outside the pub noting with pride that it is 'home of all characters and elements in James Joyce's *Finnegans Wake*', and the bridge opposite the pub has been renamed the Anna Livia Bridge.

It is the Mullingar House that perhaps holds the key to Joyce's interest in the village of Chapelizod. Joyce's father, John Stanislaus Joyce, worked in the area for three years as a young man, helping to run the short-lived Dublin Distillery Company. During this time he drank regularly at the Mullingar House, and would later tell his son a story of encountering a vagrant in the nearby Phoenix Park. While writing *Finnegans Wake* in the twenties and thirties, Joyce would tell friends that it was his father's run-in that sparked the writing of this monumental novel, prized as much for its difficulty as for its ambition and stylistic innovation.

PUBS

AND

CAFÉS

BEWLEY'S CAFÉ

78–9 Grafton Street, Dublin 2

A Dublin institution for over a century, Bewley's cafés have welcomed generations of students, shoppers, artists, writers and lovers of tea and coffee. The classic Bewley's hospitality, atmosphere and so-called 'clattery café' vibes have made them into a much-loved spot for meeting friends or reading over a cappuccino. As a result, they've had a presence in the lives of the city's authors: it was in Bewley's that Maeve Binchy would while away an afternoon listening to the conversations of her fellow Dubliners, and James Joyce mentions the café in the story 'A Little Cloud' in *Dubliners*.

Today, Bewley's Oriental Café on Grafton Street is the last existing part of the Bewley's chain, which had multiple outlets around the city at the time this flagship opened in 1927. Inside, much has remained unchanged since then. In the dark panelled back room, a row of four stained-glass windows watches over those sipping their coffee. These striking windows are the work of the artist Harry Clarke, and they were commissioned by Bewley's as a central feature on the café's opening. Even today, the atmosphere – a sort of church-like ambience amid the bustle of a busy lunch service – gives the café the feeling of a calm oasis in the busy city centre. Upstairs, a café theatre stages daily plays for those who wish to take in some culture on their lunch break. An upstairs dining room is named after James Joyce, honouring the time he spent in Bewley's, though this particular branch opened after he left Dublin for good.

THESE STAINED GLASS WINDOWS
WERE DESIGNED AND MADE
BY
HARRY CLARKE. R.H.A.
1889-1931

THIS PAGE The stained-glass windows are the outstanding feature here, while tables are also used as display space.

LEFT The 'Cruitne' window was designed by Jim Fitzpatrick.

LEFT No pub tour of the city would be complete without a visit to this Dublin institution.

BELOW LEFT The plaque certifying that the pub appears in a Joyce novel.

MULLIGAN'S

8 Poolbeg Street, Dublin 2

Dating back to 1854, Mulligan's of Poolbeg Street has earned its status as an institution for a certain kind of Dubliner. According to tradition, the elegant, old-fashioned pub has been a haven for journalists from the nearby offices of the *Irish Times* (see page 122) and the now-defunct *Irish Press*, the latter of which was based right next door until it shuttered in the nineties.

For a long time, Mulligan's also attracted a theatrical crowd, thanks to the presence of the Theatre Royal on nearby Hawkins Street, demolished in 1962. Playbills now line the wood-panelled walls in homage. These two demographics combined ensured that Mulligan's was not only a decent place to order a pint – it was also a nexus of gossip and information, making it a crucial part of Dublin's social fabric. Everyone from John F Kennedy to Judy Garland and James Joyce has passed through this storied pub, which has the feeling inside of being untouched by the passing of time. In Joyce's story 'Counterparts', from *Dubliners*, the pub is the site of a late-night arm-wrestling match between Weathers and Farrington, and now the incident is memorialized with a plaque outside.

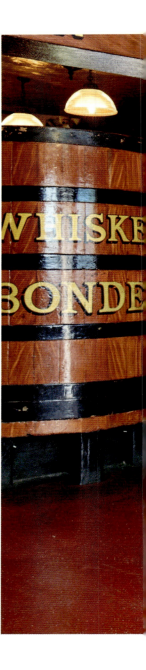

TOP AND ABOVE Mulligan's from inside and out.

LEFT A whiskey 'bonder' bought ready-distilled whiskey, then aged and bottled it to sell under their own name.

TOP AND ABOVE The snug with its claim to have inspired W.B. Yeats. Visitors may make up their own minds.

RIGHT Toners, in business since 1734.

PAGE 146: The bar area of Toner's, with Guinness on tap.

TONERS

139 Baggot Street Lower, Dublin 2

The snug at the front of Toners on Baggot Street might claim the spot of most literary feature in a Dublin pub. As a sign on the seats within explains, this is the only pub W.B. Yeats ever visited. On the urging of his fellow writer Oliver St John Gogarty, Yeats – who would have typically done his drinking in clubs or restaurants, in keeping with his social status – was brought to Toners to experience a pub first-hand. The sign in the snug goes on to say that Yeats then rose from his stool, saying, 'I have now seen a pub. I will arise and go now.' This being the first line of his poem 'The Lake Isle of Innisfree', Toners claims to be the inspiration for this poem, though most scholars would agree that this is typical pub bluster and banter.

There's no doubting Toners literary pedigree, though. Regarded by many as the quintessential Dublin pub, it has, over the years, been frequented by writers like Colm Tóibín and Patrick Kavanagh.

The light music of whisky falling into
glasses made an agreeable interlude.

JAMES JOYCE

Dubliners (1914)

THE SHELBOURNE HOTEL

27 St Stephen's Green, Dublin 2

Standing sentry at the corner of St Stephen's Green and Kildare Street, the Shelbourne Hotel occupies an important place in Dublin's history. Since the 1820s it has been regarded as one of the city's finest hotels, with its imposing façade and ever-popular Horseshoe Bar. Over the years the Shelbourne has hosted the likes of Greta Garbo, Elizabeth Taylor and Charlie Chaplin, and has been considered by many Dubliners to be one of the most glamorous and elegant addresses in the city.

Fittingly, it has played a role in Dublin's literary life too. Poets Patrick Kavanagh and Seamus Heaney frequented the Horseshoe in their time, and Edna O'Brien chose the hotel's lounge as the setting for her short story 'Send My Roots Rain', in which a librarian awaits the arrival of a distinguished poet.

In 1951, the novelist Elizabeth Bowen (see page 84) wrote a history of the hotel, an entertaining and evocative account of how the hotel came to be. It includes vivid descriptions of the action that took place at the Shelbourne during the Easter Rising of 1916, when it was occupied by the British Army, who used machine gun fire on the rebels in St Stephen's Green from a position up on the fourth floor. In the book's introduction, Bowen writes that it is the reader who will complete the book, bringing to it their own memories and ideas about the Shelbourne. Such is the hold it has over the minds of many Dubliners, past and present.

ABOVE Home to the famous Horseshoe Bar, the Shelbourne has welcomed many famous names.

OPPOSITE The hotel's imposing façade on St Stephen's Green.

LEFT The Bailey once held the famous door knocker now at the James Joyce Centre (see page 55).

THE BAILEY

1-4 Duke St, Dublin 2

The artist and one-time editor of the *Envoy* journal, John Ryan was a key figure on the scene of bohemian Dublin. Nonetheless, it was a surprise to most when he became Dublin's unlikeliest publican in 1956 after buying The Bailey on Duke Street. Under Ryan's management, The Bailey became a magnet for the McDaid's crowd (and in particular Brendan Behan, who had been barred from McDaid's for bad behaviour). Ryan detailed the goings-on of this era in his memoir *Remembering How We Stood*. First published in 1975, the author John Banville later quipped that the book would perhaps be better called *Forgetting How We Staggered*, considering the amount of alcohol imbibed by the cast of characters.

In addition to corralling this band of drinkers, Ryan was an acolyte of James Joyce and helped organize the first Bloomsday celebrations in 1954 with Flann O'Brien. When 7 Eccles Street, the fictional home of Leopold Bloom, was to be demolished in 1967, Ryan rescued the Georgian building's front door and had it installed in The Bailey. There it stood until the nineties, when it was taken to the James Joyce Centre, finally safely out of reach of any spilled pints or cigarette butts.

McDAID'S

3 Harry Street, Dublin 2

The unassuming Victorian façade of McDaid's on Harry Street gives little away. To the untrained eye, it looks like any other pub in the city centre. But in the forties and fifties, this narrow pub was the epicentre of Dublin literary culture. Built on the site of the one-time city morgue, McDaid's became a hangout for a generation of mid-century Dublin writers, of the kind who loved grumbling at the bar almost as much as they did sitting down at their desks to write. Brendan Behan, Patrick Kavanagh and Flann O'Brien all became associated with the pub on Harry Street, which also served as a secondary office for the short-lived *Envoy* journal. Edited by the artist and, later, publican, John Ryan, *Envoy* published a handful of issues between 1949 and 1951, bringing the work of Beckett, Behan, Kavanagh and even Anton Chekhov to a wider audience.

Anthony Cronin, the scene's major biographer and fellow-traveller, described the McDaid's clientele as 'layabouts, piss artists, idle rentiers, distressed gentlefolk, and dissident, breakaway or retired subversives'. Simply put, the Irish writers of this period were somewhat lost. Yeats and Joyce having recently departed, the McDaid's generation found themselves without any living writers to idolize. Modernism became a guiding light for this cohort, though that isn't to say they all got on well. Alcohol helped muddy matters, and Behan's envy of Kavanagh's rising star was palpable at the bar, with the pair often slinging barbs at each other.

Later, Seamus Heaney would launch his debut poetry collection in the pub in 1966, and a worn-down Kavanagh would speak to the younger poet only to demand a double whiskey. The layabouts and bohemians of McDaid's may have all passed on now, but their images remain on the walls, to inspire and exasperate a new generation of writers.

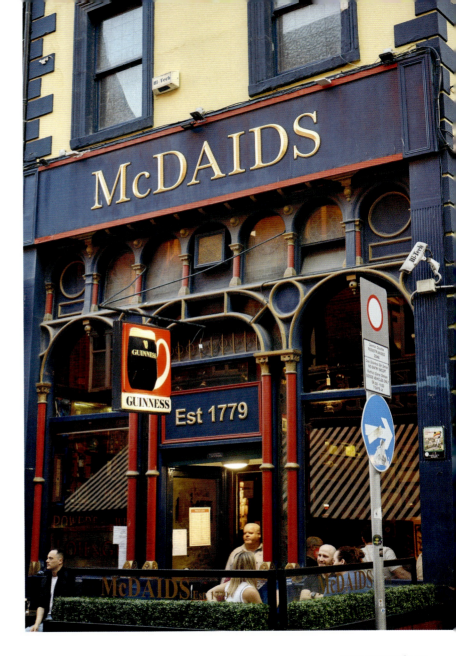

LEFT The Palace has been a journalistic and literary meeting place for over a century.

BELOW LEFT A tribute to Flann O'Brien, formerly of this parish.

THE PALACE BAR

21 Fleet Street, Dublin 2

Sitting on the edge of Temple Bar, the Palace Bar signals its literary history clearly from before you even cross its threshold. Look down to the pavement outside and you'll see the names of some of the pub's illustrious drinkers of the past set in bronze. The Palace's backstory contains many of the most prominent writers in Dublin's history, as well as countless unnamed hangers-on. During the forties and fifties, the narrow mahogany and oak bar here attracted the likes of Flann O'Brien, Brendan Behan and Patrick Kavanagh, who described the place as 'the most wonderful temple of art'.

The story goes that the writers arrived at the Palace because it was where R.M. Smyllie, then the editor of the *Irish Times*, liked to drink. At the time, the paper had a weekly literary page for which Smyllie commissioned poems and paid £1 each for them. In the pleasant high-ceilinged backroom of the pub, it is easy to imagine Dublin's poets competing for the editor's attentions. Smyllie's near-daily presence kept writers coming back and also drew a regular crowd of journalists from the paper's nearby offices

A young Edna O'Brien also frequented the Palace, hoping to encounter the literati of the city. In her memoir, *Country Girl*, she wrote of finding Kavanagh 'boorish', and of spotting Smyllie wearing a green sombrero and yellow waistcoat, merrily editing his articles at the bar before last orders.

LEFT AND TOP Floral displays compete for attention with painted lamps outside.

ABOVE Original woodwork with partitions for private conversation.

OPPOSITE The landlord's name lives on in *Ulysses*; the original Davy Byrne ended up as a character in the novel.

RIGHT Stop here on the Joycean literary trail – the pub will gladly make you the exact lunch that Leopold Bloom ate here.

DAVY BYRNES

21 Duke Street, Dublin 2

Davy Byrnes is perhaps the Dublin pub most closely associated with James Joyce, thanks to its cameo appearance in the 'Lestrygonians' episode of *Ulysses*. Describing it as a 'moral pub', Leopold Bloom pops by for a gorgonzola sandwich with 'pungent mustard' and accompanied by a glass of burgundy. The publican Davy Byrne himself features in this section, turning him into an unlikely literary celebrity in Dublin life.

Accordingly, Joyce was also a regular at Davy Byrnes, and in a 1962 interview with the *Irish Times*, the barman John Power who served him revealed that Joyce's drink of choice was unusual: a mixture of brandy and orange Curaçao. Today, those who celebrate Bloomsday on 16 June stop by Davy Byrnes around 2pm to recreate the Ulysses pitstop, with wine and a cheese sandwich, à La Bloom.

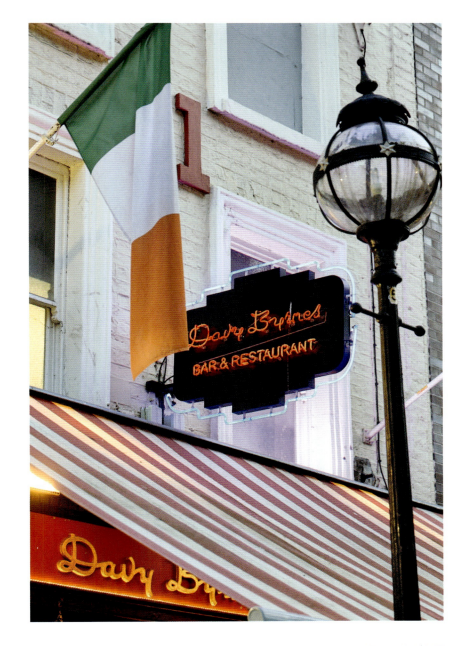

LEFT This is the place to come for a pre- or post-theatre drink: the Abbey Theatre is round the corner.

OPPOSITE The Easter Rising may have been planned here; the original hotel on this site was burned down in 1916 during the fighting.

WYNN'S HOTEL

35–9 Abbey Street, Dublin 1

With its distinctive and old-fashioned sign hanging outside, this family-run hotel on Abbey Street has held a pivotal place in the history of the city since its opening in 1845. The close proximity of Wynn's Hotel to the Abbey Theatre (see page 38) has given it a special status in the city's cultural history. Lady Gregory and W.B. Yeats often stayed at the hotel during their time at the Abbey. In the early twentieth century, the hotel was also used by the rebels of the Easter Rising to hold planning meetings. During the Rising, it was burned to the ground amid fierce fighting on the street outside. Rebuilding began in 1921 and Wynn's reopened its doors in 1926, ready to welcome a new era in the capital.

Today it has a loyal group of customers, thanks to its storied past, and is often favoured by Irish visitors from outside Dublin on their trips to the city. Literature and history are never far away at Wynn's, and in the hotel's Saints and Scholars bar, colourful stained-glass panels behind the bar feature likenesses of Irish writers including James Joyce, Yeats, Pádraig Pearse and Samuel Beckett.

THE DUKE

9 Duke Street, Dublin 2

Established in 1822, the pub now known as the Duke has held many names over the years but inside, much of its traditional Victorian interiors remain to this day. Its longevity, as well as its convenient location just off Grafton Street, have made the Duke into a Dublin institution. With that comes many claims to literary history, and like many historic Dublin pubs, it is said that Joyce, Behan and Kavanagh all drank here at various points.

Letters from Joyce are framed and hung on the wall, and the nightly Dublin Literary Pub Crawl sets off from here. This popular tour is as much about street theatre as it is about imbibing, with actors bringing to life scenes from both the city's novels and its literary history. The Duke is also a regular site for book launch after-parties, thanks to its close proximity to Hodges Figgis (see page 20) next door.

BIBLIOGRAPHY

Banville, John, *Time Pieces: A Dublin Memoir* (Ireland: Hachette Books Ireland, 2016).

Berryman, John, *The Dream Songs*, 'Dream Song 312' (New York: Farrar, Straus & Giroux, 2007).

Boland, Eavan, *A Poet's Dublin*, introduction 'City of Shadows', ed. Paula Meehan and Jody Allen Randolph (Manchester: Carcanet, 2014).

Bowen, Elizabeth, *Seven Winters: Memories of a Dublin Childhood* (London: Longmans, Green & Co, 1943).

Cronin, Anthony, *No Laughing Matter: The Life and Times of Flann O'Brien* (Dublin: New Island Books, 2019).

McGahern, John, *Memoir* (London: Faber & Faber, 2005).

O'Brien, Edna, *Country Girl: A Memoir* (London: Faber & Faber, 2013).

Wall, Richard, *Wittgenstein in Ireland* (London: Reaktion Books, 2000).

Wilde, Oscar, *Lady Windermere's Fan* (London: Penguin Books, 2011).

Pavilion
An imprint of HarperCollins*Publishers* Ltd
1 London Bridge Street
London SE1 9GF

www.harpercollins.co.uk

HarperCollins*Publishers*
Macken House
39/40 Mayor Street Upper
Dublin 1, D01 C9W8
Ireland

10 9 8 7 6 5 4 3 2 1

First published in Great Britain by
Pavilion, an imprint of HarperCollins*Publishers* Ltd 2025
Copyright © Ana Kinsella 2025
Images © Killian Broderick 2025
Images on p108-111 with the permission of
the Board of Trinity College Dublin.

Ana Kinsella asserts the moral right to
be identified as the author of this work.
A catalogue record for this book is available from the British Library.

ISBN 978-0-00-8716-097

FSC
www.fsc.org

MIX
Paper | Supporting
responsible forestry
FSC™ C007454

This book is produced from independently certified FSC™ paper
to ensure responsible forest management.

For more information visit:
www.harpercollins.co.uk/green

Printed and bound in China

Publishing Director: Laura Russell
Commissioning Editor: Ellen Simmons
Designer: Lily Wilson
Layout Designer: Cara Rogers
Copy editor: Sarah Prior
Captioning: Clare Double
Proofreader: Kathy Woolley
Production controller: Grace O'Byrne